BUT, CHANCELLOR

BUT, CHANCELLOR

by Hugo Young and Anne Sloman

British Broadcasting Corporation

Published by the British Broadcasting Corporation,
35 Marylebone High Street, London W1M 4AA

ISBN 0 563 20237 8   Hardback
ISBN 0 563 20238 6   Paperback
First published 1984
© The contributors and the British Broadcasting Corporation 1984

Set in 10/12 Linotron Palatino by Input Typesetting Limited
and printed in England by Hartnolls Ltd, Bodmin, Cornwall
Cover/jacket printed by George Over Ltd, Rugby, Warwickshire

Contents

Preface

The radio series on which this book is based grew out of an earlier series, also preserved in print, called *No, Minister*.[1] *No, Minister* established the precedent for *But, Chancellor*, not least in respect of the conditions under which the programmes were put together. Once again, it is important to make clear what these conditions were.

Before *No, Minister*, which broke new ground by putting civil servants on the air to talk about their work and life in Whitehall, a lengthy correspondence was necessary between the BBC and the then Civil Service Department to agree the ground-rules which would govern the making of the programmes. The exchange of letters is recorded in the *No, Minister* book. The same rules were accepted by the Treasury for *But, Chancellor*. In essence, they stipulated that while any interviewee could decline to answer any question without his refusal being broadcast, and while he could withdraw or alter anything he said, this could only be done before the formal ending of the interview (a safety net which was in fact only used on one occasion by a minister and on another by a non-Treasury contributor who had each made a minor factual error in one answer). Once we had left his (or her) room, the material on tape was the property of the BBC, to be used or omitted at our unfettered discretion. Likewise, although the general areas to be covered by the programmes were decided only after discussions with Treasury officials, control over their final content was ours alone. No one in the Treasury heard any programme before it was broadcast.

To this impeccable respect for the freedom of journalism there were, inevitably, one or two limits set. One was a polite form of surveillance. Most conversations in Whitehall, and especially in the Treasury, are in some way minuted, and it would have been a break with tradition if the institution had made no attempt to monitor what we were doing. A 'minder' was supplied to accompany us to each interview and record it on his own machine. We took this to be part of an earnest

---

1 *No, Minister*, by Hugo Young and Anne Sloman, BBC Publications, 1982.

attempt, characteristic of government press offices the world over, to guard against unwitting disagreements between one civil servant and another, to the possible scandal of the public outside. What happened to these parallel recordings remained, however, a mystery. We met no one who confessed to hearing the earlier tapes, and hardly anyone who would have had time to do so. And by the end of our journey through the red-linoed corridors of Great George Street, the minder's attendance had become markedly less constant.

A more substantial constraint arose from the choice of people to interview. Inevitably, this lay mostly with the Treasury itself. A range of names was discussed between us, bearing in mind the two criteria of fluent speaking and relevance to our themes. The most senior officials were obvious choices anyway. But beyond the top handful, the names put forward had the personal imprimatur of the then Permanent Secretary, Sir Douglas Wass. All were volunteers. They were told, we later learned, that their careers 'would not be jeopardised if they chose not to volunteer'! Clearly, by this method the Treasury ensured that it put on its best performers. But this did not benefit the Treasury alone. Self-confident speakers invariably make for better listening than stumbling, reluctant ones. We came across a few of these and, having a plethora of material, used few of their words. None showed any sign of having been schooled in the routine response, although Sir Douglas did call them to a meeting before our arrival. It seems to have been a less than solemn occasion. 'If there were any guidelines, I'm sure everybody forgot them the moment they walked out of the room,' one participant said. According to another, there was 'a certain amount of scurrilous joking as to what the common link between us was'. The only theme that seems to have been urged on them was the need to play down their own importance, and recall at frequent intervals that ministers, not civil servants, are responsible for what the Treasury does. In our experience no Whitehall official ever needs to be reminded about this disclaimer. For public purposes it is built into their bones from the earliest years.

The text in this book is substantially longer than the programmes as they were broadcast. The shape of the five programmes is the same and all the words broadcast are retained – without any updating to take account of subsequent economic developments or changes of post. (It is a revealing aspect of Treasury life that half the people we interviewed for the programmes had changed their jobs before this book went to press, less than six months later.[1]) But we conducted more than forty interviews and much useful material had to be left out of the half-hour broadcasts. In the less constrained span of a book it would have been a pity not to cull the interviews further. Since the main purpose of putting this particular radio series into print is to put on permanent record the utterances – still rare, even today – of serving civil servants, we thought we had a duty to let nothing of value escape. We envisage the book being, if nothing else, material worth quarrying by more scholarly analysts of British administration.

For better or worse, *But, Chancellor*, like *No, Minister*, is peculiarly a piece of radio journalism. It would not have been possible in a newspaper, still less on television. It is simply not conceivable that the Treasury would have opened its doors so freely to either writers or cameramen. Why? One part of the answer may be that they would not have been trusted to tell the truth. If this is so, it immediately throws light on both the strength and the weakness of radio journalism. Its strength is its immediacy: the opportunity it gives otherwise reticent people to put down for the record their very own words, unvarnished and as they chose to say them. If they speak to writing journalists, they can never be so sure of being accurately represented as they would like to be. If they go on television, they fear the medium will altogether overshadow the message and probably distort it. On radio, ideas can be explored without distraction. People who speak to the microphone – and trust the good faith of producer and writer – know at least that their words cannot be interfered with. Thus, in a sense, while conceding editorial control to the BBC, the mandarins remained more in charge of the way they were to be presented than they would be in any other medium. Which underlines, of course, radio's limitation, and its inescapable weakness. It is wholly dependent on what people are willing to say. The inferences, allusions and off-the-record statements on which print journalism thrives are mostly denied to the radio reporter. The world he displays is, to a considerable extent, the world as depicted for public display by its own occupants.

The interviews were recorded between mid-November 1982

---

1 *See* the Treasury Organisation chart on p. 18 for some examples.

and mid-February 1983. The interviews in the Postscript, containing some reactions to the programmes both from participants in them and from elsewhere in Whitehall, took place in June and July 1983. For expediting the series, we owe some debts of gratitude. Within the Treasury we thank especially Sir Douglas Wass, who seemed to communicate to many of his staff his own enthusiasm for the project. We also thank Martin Hall, head of the Treasury Information Division, for his help. At the BBC we are warmly grateful to Chris Garrett, who handled all administration of the series, Rosemary Edgerley, for her research assistance, and Janet Smith, for so efficiently producing the manuscript.

Hugo Young
Anne Sloman
1 September 1983

The Participants

Airey, Sir Lawrence
b. 1926. *Educ.* Newcastle Royal Grammar School; Cambridge.
Entered civil service 1949. Joined Treasury 1958: Under
Secretary 1969–73; Deputy Secretary 1973–7; Second
Permanent Secretary 1977–9. Chairman of the Board of Inland
Revenue 1980– .

Anson, John
b. 1930. *Educ.* Winchester; Cambridge. Entered Treasury 1954.
Economic Minister, British Embassy, Washington and UK
Executive Director, IMF and World Bank 1980–3. Deputy
Secretary responsible for industry 1983– .

Bailey, Alan
b. 1931. *Educ.* Bedford School; Oxford. Entered Treasury 1956.
Deputy Secretary 1978–83. Seconded to be Deputy Head of
CPRS 1981–2. Second Permanent Secretary in charge of public
services 1983– .

Beckett, Sir Terence
b. 1923. *Educ.* London School of Economics. Managing
Director and Chief Executive of Ford Motor Co. Ltd 1974–80,
Chairman 1976–80. Director General of Confederation of
British Industry 1980– .

Benn, Rt Hon. Tony
b. 1925. *Educ.* Westminster School; Oxford. Labour MP
1950–60, 63–83. Postmaster General 1964–6. Minister of
Technology 1966–70. Secretary of State for Industry 1974–5.
Secretary of State for Energy 1975–9.

Brittan, Rt Hon. Leon
b. 1939. *Educ.* Haberdashers Aske's School; Cambridge; Yale.
Conservative MP 1974– . Minister of State at the Home
Office 1979–81. Chief Secretary to the Treasury 1981–3. Home
Secretary 1983– .

Britton, Andrew
b. 1940. *Educ.* Royal Grammar School, Newcastle-upon-Tyne;
Oxford; London School of Economics. Entered Treasury 1966.

Under Secretary at the Treasury 1980–2. Director of the
National Institute of Economic and Social Research 1982– .

Bryars, Desmond
b. 1928. *Educ.* St Edward's School, Oxford; Oxford. Entered
Air Ministry 1952. Treasury 1960. Deputy Under Secretary
(Finance and Budget) at the Ministry of Defence 1979– .

Burns, Sir Terence
b. 1944. *Educ.* Houghton-le-Spring Grammar School;
Manchester University. Joined London Business School 1965.
Director of LBS Centre for Economic Forecasting 1977.
Professor of Economics 1979. Joined Treasury as Chief
Economic Adviser 1980.

Butt, Richard
b. 1943. *Educ.* Westcliff High School; Oxford. Ministry of
Housing 1965–8. University Research Fellow and Consultant
1969–72. Entered Treasury 1973. Seconded to UK Permanent
Representation to the European Communities as Financial
Counsellor 1981– .

Camdessus, Michel
b. 1933. *Educ.* Collège Notre-Dame de Betharram; Faculté de
droit de Paris. Censeur du Crédit national 1982. Directeur du
Trésor 1982– .

Cooper, Sir Frank
b. 1922. *Educ.* Manchester Grammar School; Oxford. Assistant
Principal at the Air Ministry 1948. Permanent Under
Secretary at the Ministry of Defence 1976–82.

Cropper, Peter
b. 1927. *Educ.* Hitchin Grammar School; Cambridge.
Conservative Research Department 1951–3, 1975–9.
Stockbroking, Investment Analysis, Portfolio Management
1953–75. Special Adviser to the Chancellor 1979–82. Director
of the Conservative Research Department 1982– .

George, Edward
b. 1938. *Educ.* Dulwich College; Cambridge. Joined Bank of
England 1962. Seconded to the International Monetary Fund
1972–4. Executive Director of the Bank of England 1982– .

Gilmore, Brian
b. 1937. *Educ.* Wolverhampton Grammar School; Oxford.

Entered Commonwealth Relations Office 1958. Principal of the Civil Service College 1979–81. Principal Establishment and Finance Officer at the Treasury 1982– .

Godber, Stephen
b. 1950. *Educ.* Bedford School; Lancaster University. Entered the Department of Health and Social Security 1973. On secondment to the Treasury as Principal of the Local Government Division 1981–3.

Gold, Sir Joseph
b. 1912. *Educ.* London University; Harvard. British Mission, Washington DC. 1942–6. Joined the International Monetary Fund 1946. Senior Consultant IMF 1979– .

Hancock, David
b. 1934. *Educ.* Whitgift School; Oxford. Assistant Principal at the Board of Trade 1957. Transferred to the Treasury 1959. Deputy Secretary at the Office of the UK Permanent Representative to the European Communities, Brussels 1980–2. Deputy Secretary at the Cabinet Office 1982–3. Permanent Secretary at the Department of Education and Science 1983– .

Healey, Rt Hon. Denis
b. 1917. *Educ.* Bradford Grammar School; Oxford. Labour MP 1952– . Secretary of State for Defence 1964–70. Chancellor of the Exchequer 1974–9. Opposition spokesman on the Treasury 1979–81, on Foreign Affairs 1981– . Deputy Leader of the Labour Party 1980–3.

Howe, Rt Hon. Sir Geoffrey
b. 1926. *Educ.* Winchester; Cambridge. Conservative MP 1964–6; 1970– . Solicitor-General 1970–2. Minister for Trade and Consumer Affairs 1972–4. Chancellor of the Exchequer 1979–83. Foreign Secretary 1983– .

Hulme, Geoffrey
b. 1931. *Educ.* King's School, Macclesfield; Oxford. Joined Ministry of Health 1953. Assistant Secretary 1967–74; Under Secretary 1974–81. Deputy Secretary and Principal Finance Officer at the DHSS 1981– .

Jenkins, Rt Hon. Roy
b. 1920. *Educ.* Abersychan Grammar School; Oxford. Labour

MP 1948–76. Minister of Aviation 1964–5. Home Secretary 1965–7, 1974–6. Chancellor of the Exchequer 1967–70. Deputy Leader of the Labour Party 1970–2. President of the European Commission 1977–81. Social Democrat MP 1982– . First Leader of the SDP 1982–3.

Kelley, Joan
b. 1926. *Educ.* Whalley Range High School, Manchester; London School of Economics. Entered Cabinet Office 1949. Under Secretary in the Treasury in charge of the Home, Education and Transport Group 1981– .

Kemp, Peter
b. 1934. *Educ.* Royal Naval College, Dartmouth. Chartered accountant 1959. Entered Ministry of Transport 1967. Transferred to the Treasury 1973. Under Secretary at the Treasury 1978– .

Lea, David
b. 1937. *Educ.* Farnham Grammar School; Cambridge. Joined Economist Intelligence Unit 1961. Joined the Economic Department of the Trades Union Congress 1964. Assistant General Secretary of the TUC 1977– .

Lever, Paul
b. 1944. *Educ.* St Paul's School; Oxford. Joined Commonwealth Office 1966. Third Secretary, Helsinki 1967, UK delegation to NATO 1971. First Secretary Foreign and Commonwealth Office 1973. Assistant Private Secretary to the Foreign Secretary 1978–81. *Chef de Cabinet* to Christopher Tugendhat, EC Commission, Brussels 1981– .

Littler, Geoffrey
b. 1930. *Educ.* Manchester Grammar School; Cambridge. Entered the Colonial Office 1952. Transferred to the Treasury 1954. Under Secretary at the Treasury 1972, Deputy Secretary 1977, Second Permanent Secretary (Overseas Finance) 1983– .

Loehnis, Anthony
b. 1936. *Educ.* Eton; Oxford; Harvard. Diplomatic Service 1960–6. Associate Director of the Bank of England 1980–1. Executive Director of the Bank of England 1981– .

Lomax, Rachel
b. 1945. *Educ.* Cheltenham Ladies College; Cambridge; London School of Economics. Entered the Treasury 1968. Senior Economic Adviser 1978– , in Macro-economic Policy Division 1981–3. Assistant Secretary Monetary Policy Division 1983– .

Meacher, Michael
b. 1939. *Educ.* Berkhamsted School; Oxford. Labour MP 1970– . Parliamentary Under Secretary of State at the Department of Industry 1974–5; DHSS 1976–7; Department of Trade 1976–9. Chairman of sub-committee of Treasury Select Committee.

Middleton, Peter
b. 1934. *Educ.* Sheffield City Grammar School; Sheffield University; Bristol University. Entered the Treasury 1964. Private Secretary to the Chancellor 1969–72. Treasury Press Secretary 1972–5. Head of Monetary Policy Division 1975; Under Secretary 1976. Deputy Secretary (Domestic Economy) 1980–3. Permanent Secretary 1983– .

Monck, Nicholas
b. 1935. *Educ.* Eton; Cambridge. Ministry of Power 1959–62. Transferred to the Treasury 1969. Private Secretary to the Chancellor 1976–7. Under Secretary (Nationalised Industries) 1977–80, (Home Finance) 1980– .

Monger, George
b. 1937. *Educ.* Holloway School; Cambridge. Entered Home Civil Service 1961. Ministry of Power, Department of Trade and Industry, Department of Energy 1961–81. Under Secretary at the Treasury 1981– .

Norgrove, David
b. 1948. *Educ.* Oxford; London School of Economics. Entered the Treasury 1974. On secondment to the First National Bank of Chicago 1978–80. Principal in the Central Unit 1981– .

Posner, Michael
b. 1931. *Educ.* Whitgift School; Oxford. Fellow Pembroke College, Cambridge 1960– . Economic Adviser to the Treasury 1967–9, Economic Consultant 1969–71. Consultant to the International Monetary Fund 1971–2. Deputy Chief

Economic Adviser to the Treasury 1975–6. Chairman of the
Social Science Research Council 1979–83.

Priestley, Clive
b. 1935. *Educ.* Loughborough Grammar School; Nottingham
University. Entered the Home Civil Service 1960. Chief of
Staff to Sir Derek Rayner in the Prime Minister's Office
1979–82. Under Secretary in the Management and Personnel
Office 1982–3. Director of Special Projects at British Telecom
1983– .

Rawlinson, Sir Anthony
b. 1926. *Educ.* Eton; Oxford. Entered the Ministry of Labour
and National Service 1951. Transferred to the Treasury 1953.
Economic Minister at the British Embassy, Washington and
UK Director of the International Monetary Fund and World
Bank 1972–5. Deputy Secretary at the Department of Industry
1975, Second Permanent Secretary 1976. Second Permanent
Secretary (Public Services) at the Treasury 1977–83. Permanent
Secretary at the Department of Trade 1983– .

Regan, Donald
b. 1918. *Educ.* Cambridge Latin School; Harvard. Merrill
Lynch, Pierce, Fenner and Smith Inc. 1946–81, Chairman of
the Board 1973–81. Secretary of the Treasury, US Treasury
Department 1981– .

Sallnow-Smith, Nicholas
b. 1950. *Educ.* Hastings Grammar School; Cambridge. Entered
the Treasury 1975. Private Secretary to the Permanent
Secretary 1978–9. Principal (Higher Education) 1979–83.
Seconded to Manufacturers, Hanover Trust Company
1983– .

Seammen, Diana
b. 1948. *Educ.* Apsley Grammar School; Macclesfield High
School; Sussex University. Entered the Treasury 1969.
Seconded to S. G. Warburg and Co. Ltd 1979–82. Assistant
Secretary (Social Services and Territorial Division) 1982– .

Shore, Rt Hon. Peter
b. 1924. *Educ.* Quarry Bank High School, Liverpool;
Cambridge. Labour MP 1964– . Secretary of State for
Economic Affairs 1967–9. Secretary of State for Trade 1974–6.
Secretary of State for the Environment 1976–9. Opposition

spokesman on Foreign Affairs 1979–80, on Treasury and Economic Affairs 1980– .

Stowe, Sir Kenneth
b. 1927. *Educ.* Dagenham County High School; Oxford. Assistant Principal at the National Assistance Board 1951. Financial Counsellor at the British Embassy, Washington and UK Director of the International Monetary Fund 1965–7. Under Secretary at the Treasury 1968, Deputy Secretary 1970–3, Second Permanent Secretary 1973–4. Assistant Secretary Department of Health and Social Security 1970–3. Under Secretary at the Cabinet Office 1973–5, Deputy Secretary 1976. Principal Private Secretary to the Prime Minister 1975–9. Permanent Secretary at the Northern Ireland Office 1979–81. Permanent Secretary at the DHSS 1981– .

Tugendhat, Christopher
b. 1937. *Educ.* Ampleforth College; Cambridge. Conservative MP 1970–6. Opposition spokesman on Employment 1974–5, on Foreign and Commonwealth Affairs 1975–6. Member of the Commission of European Communities 1977– , Vice President 1981– .

Walsh, Harry
b. 1939. *Educ.* McGill University, Montreal; Cambridge. Entered the Treasury 1966. Private Secretary to the Chancellor of the Duchy of Lancaster 1974–6. Member of the Cabinet Office Secretariat 1978–80. Economic Counsellor at the British Embassy, Washington 1980– .

Wass, Sir Douglas
b. 1923. *Educ.* Nottingham High School; Cambridge. Entered the Treasury 1946. Private Secretary to the Chancellor 1959–61, to the Chief Secretary 1961–2. Permanent Secretary at the Treasury 1974–83. Joint Head of the Civil Service 1982–3.

1 January 1983   HM TREASURY ORGANISATION CHART

	Deputy Secretaries (6)	Under Secretaries (23)	Assistant Secretaries (71)	Principals (149)
RT HON SIR GEOFFREY HOWE QC MP *Chancellor of the Exchequer*		PETER KEMP		DAVID NORGROVE
		BRIAN GILMORE		
RT HON LEON BRITTAN QC MP *Chief Secretary*	*Deputy Secretary Pay & Allowances*			
Financial Secretary	TERENCE BURNS *Chief Economic Adviser*		RACHEL LOMAX	
Economic Secretary				
Minister of State (Civil Service)	*Deputy Chief Economic Adviser*			
Minister of State (Revenue)	ALAN BAILEY *Deputy Secretary Industry*			
	PETER MIDDLETON *Deputy Secretary Public Finance*	NICHOLAS MONCK		
SIR DOUGLAS WASS GCB *Permanent Secretary*	*Deputy Secretary Overseas Finance*			
GEOFFREY LITTLER *2nd Permanent Secretary Overseas Finance Sector*	*Deputy Secretary General Expenditure*	GEORGE MONGER	DIANA SEAMMEN	STEPHEN GODBER
SIR ANTHONY RAWLINSON KCB *2nd Permanent Secretary Public Services Sector*		JOAN KELLEY		NICHOLAS SALLNOW-SMITH

HM TREASURY ORGANISATION

SIR GEOFFREY HOWE became Foreign Secretary on 11 June 1983 after the general election, and was succeeded as Chancellor by Nigel Lawson.

LEON BRITTAN became Home Secretary on 11 June 1983 and was succeeded by Peter Rees.

SIR DOUGLAS WASS retired in March 1983 and was succeeded by PETER MIDDLETON.

SIR ANTHONY RAWLINSON left the Treasury to become Permanent Secretary at the Department of Trade on 28 April 1983. He was replaced by ALAN BAILEY, who in turn was replaced by John Anson. John Anson doesn't appear on this chart as the post of Economic Minister in Washington, which he held when he contributed to the programmes, counts as a secondment to the Diplomatic Service.

PETER KEMP was promoted to Deputy Secretary in charge of the Pay and Allowances sector on 15 April 1983.

GEORGE MONGER remained as Under Secretary but moved to the Fiscal Policy Division on 27 June 1983.

RACHEL LOMAX remained as Assistant Secretary but moved to the Monetary Policy Division on 9 May 1983.

NICK SALLNOW-SMITH left for a two-year secondment to the bankers, Manufacturers Hanover Trust, on 14 February 1983.

STEPHEN GODBER completed his secondment to the Treasury from the DHSS on 18 March 1983.

The Topmost Mandarins

First Broadcast: 27 February 1983

Mandarins were originally Chinese. The term describes a superior public official. But in our language mandarins live in Whitehall, and it is in Her Majesty's Treasury, at the bottom of Whitehall, that the British mandarin finds his supreme incarnation. The image – used with a mixture of awe and faintly sardonic disrespect – is very special. In the mythology, Treasury mandarins are powerful, yet silky smooth; influential but strangely unknown; clever, devious, inscrutable and not a little self-satisfied. It is the work of these paragons which *But, Chancellor* sets out to explore, using, for the first time, their own voices to do so. Later we will be looking at how they control public spending, going behind the scenes of the Budget process, which culminates in a fortnight's time. We will also be looking at one of the less visible aspects of the Treasury's work – its continuing post-imperial role in the world economy. At the end, we will hear from them how much blame they take for the state of the British economy. But we begin by trying to demystify the mandarins themselves.

How this title for the series came about offers a first lesson in wisdom. It was to have been called *Please, Chancellor*, to locate the Treasury, as we thought, in its proper place in Whitehall, beset by applicants on every side for higher public spending or lower private taxes. It was Sir Douglas Wass, Permanent Secretary and chief of mandarins,[1] who warned us off: *But, Chancellor* would be more aptly symbolic – the key phrase on the lips of every well-trained Treasury civil servant, conveying the deference, yet the relentlessness, of the advice it is his job to submit to ministers. Nor, it would be as well to establish from the start, does this advice in fact come from an easily defined Treasury type – someone you would recognise as a mandarin. Start with a view from outside. Clive Priestley, as head of the Civil Service Efficiency Unit[2] and not a Treasury man, observes the place from a well situated eyrie: and smooth is not always the word.

1 Sir Douglas Wass retired as Permanent Secretary on 31 March 1983 and was succeeded by Peter Middleton.
2 Clive Priestley left the civil service in July 1983 to become Director of Special Projects at British Telecom.

Priestley:

I'm not sure what a Treasury mandarin is – I mean, most people outside the service tend to think in terms of bowler hats, black jackets and pinstripe trousers. My own feeling is that the Treasury is not actually very much like that. My own experience is that it has got a large number of both hairy and smooth men. It has also got a third category of person, namely saintly men – and indeed, women as well – and I think it would be very difficult to characterise them all under the term 'mandarin'.

Hairy, smooth or saintly, Treasury people also quite clearly have an *esprit de corps*, which Roy Jenkins, Chancellor of the Exchequer from 1967 to 1970, obviously has not forgotten on his journey, via the European Commission, to the leadership of the SDP.[1]

Jenkins:

There is a certain special ethos about the Treasury which I suppose some people might regard as a bad thing. I don't, as a matter of fact. In a way it's a very egalitarian society that regards itself almost as part of an élite. Compared with the Home Office, certainly the Home Office which I first knew in the sixties,[2] it was a very non-hierarchical society. Everybody in what was then called the Administrative Grade was supposed to call each other by their Christian names. For example, my third Private Secretary was supposed to call the Permanent Secretary by his Christian name, which he found rather difficult to do in some ways.

It actually now seems to come quite naturally. We didn't hear anyone referring to the Permanent Secretary other than as Douglas.[3] Such un-British familiarity is owed at least in part to the fact that the Treasury is quite extraordinarily small. Fewer than 350 officials at the rank of Principal and above run the whole of British economic policy: something which strikes exchange visitors from a department like Health and Social Security, which has over 90,000 staff, with great force. Stephen Godber, on secondment from the DHSS, is, at thirty-three, a Principal in charge of monitoring public spending on housing.[4]

---

1 Roy Jenkins stood down as leader of the SDP in June 1983.
2 Roy Jenkins was Labour Home Secretary from 1965 to 1967 and from 1974 to 1976.
3 Sir Douglas Wass.
4 Stephen Godber returned to the DHSS in March 1983.

Godber:

It's much more likely for a Principal in the Treasury to find himself hauled up to see a minister or the Chief Secretary at short notice or to provide briefing direct to the Chief Secretary at short notice than would be the case in the DHSS. And that, I find, is quite satisfying because it does mean that if I'm the person who's paid to know most about housing in the Treasury, I'm probably the one who actually delivers the advice direct to the minister.

This sense of intimacy is intensified by the fact that all the civil servants in the Treasury appear to know each other very well. Joan Kelley is an Under Secretary who joined the service in 1949.

Kelley:

I was looking, just before you came, at the organisation chart[1] and I think I know everybody on this chart bar some of the recently appointed economic forecasters, and people like that, whom I don't have to deal with personally. Some of these people I've known for twenty-five years and we can of course communicate with each other almost in code.

This almost-private coterie, according to another Principal, David Norgrove, who spent two years outside the Treasury at the First National Bank of Chicago, forms itself into a textbook embodiment of unbiased judgement.

Norgrove:

I think the thing that's really impressed me is, firstly, how people try to be as independent and objective as they possibly can, and secondly, the degree of loyalty they have towards the ministers who are in power to help them try to achieve what they want. I'm not bullshitting about that – I think that's exactly what I've seen. That's not to say that officials don't have views which may sometimes differ from those of the minister's – you'd hardly expect anyone worth their salt not to have their own views about the kinds of problems we face – but that doesn't mean to say that they don't try their hardest not to let those views influence the kind of advice they give and the way in which they try to put the policies into effect.

We'll come back to this question of objective advice and how it marries up with the views of civil servants later on. Meanwhile,

---

1 *See* p. 18.

there's no doubt that, whatever its objectivity, the advice Treasury ministers get from officials comes almost invariably from very clever people – clever, moreover, in ways and styles which redefine the image of the mandarin from that smooth-tongued inscrutable of Chinese legend to something a lot rougher, more argumentative – behind closed doors – than you'd ever imagine from the outside. Michael Posner, Cambridge don and economic adviser to Labour ministers for twenty years, has no doubt about the Treasury's special brand of cleverness.

Posner:

The Treasury has always been the power-house. Harold Lever[1] once said that moving to the Treasury from another department was like coming to the Savoy from a two-star hotel out in the provinces. I wouldn't want to be unfair to other departments, I've worked in several outside the Treasury and I love them and they're very important, but the Treasury has always contained very clever people, at least as clever as one meets at High Table in an average Oxbridge college. They're well read, they're accomplished, they're intelligent, they're knowledgeable, they're powerful – it's an immensely exciting environment.

Although it is also, according to Michael Meacher, a very young junior minister in the second Wilson government, one in which a certain arrogance flourishes.

Meacher:

As a very callow minister back in 1974–5[2] I had a rather good idea and put it forward, and there was a pause and a very dry response from the other side: 'Well, if you think it's such a good idea, minister, why do you think we wouldn't have thought of it first?'

The thirst for honest argument is what has impressed Terry Burns, brought in from the London Business School by Sir Geoffrey Howe as Chief Economic Adviser when he was only thirty-seven.

Burns:

You don't get any sense, in terms of discussions or arguments, of people attempting to win their point by trying to

---

1 Harold Lever (Lord Lever of Manchester 1979–) was Labour MP 1945–79, Financial Secretary to the Treasury 1967–9, Paymaster General 1969–70, and Chancellor of the Duchy of Lancaster 1974–9.
2 Parliamentary Under Secretary, Department of Industry 1974–5.

argue 'I'm a cleverer chap than you'. Life is very much based upon the quality of the argument and upon the issues. It is the issues and the arguments that are the matters of consideration, rather than the personalities or in a sense one-upmanship, in terms of individuals' personal or intellectual characteristics.

All the Treasury high-fliers we spoke to made a lot of this tradition of internal argument. Nicholas Monck, for example, has been Private Secretary to several ministers and is now Under Secretary in charge of the Home Finance group.

Monck:

An important part of the ethos, I would say, is allowing dissent, and allowing dissent to reach ministers. If you want to exercise the right to disagree you can, and it is often used and I think that is a very good thing. It isn't a very hierarchical organisation, you get quite violent arguments of an intellectual kind, up and down and sideways between all the different bits of the Treasury.

Even much more junior officials, like David Norgrove, a Principal in the Central Unit, feel free to put in their two bits' worth.

Norgrove:

I have no hesitation at all about saying anything if I think it is worth saying, and I think in the vast majority of cases it would be listened to regardless of where it comes from. That's one of the great attractions of the Treasury. I think to some extent it's a difference from some of the private sector companies I've come across, too.

Another distinguishing characteristic, of course, is the paper-work – reams, files, tons of it – and the meetings which endlessly precede and flow from it. It's all a far cry from the common-rooms and think-tanks Terry Burns is used to.

Burns:

People do write down a great deal more than in any organisation I have seen but that is a personal characteristic, of course, of the civil service. I think it is also a characteristic of a department which is trying to keep a large number of people in touch with each issue, because it is doing this co-ordinating role and that means that you have to have some way of dispersing information fairly widely. You see the same characteristic in meetings. Meetings, typically, are very large. At the Chancellor's meetings you see an awful lot of people, a good number of whom will not be speaking. In a sense they will be there in the role of observers or spectators, because they're the people who will then have to go out and make sure that what has been decided on is put into place, and they regard the best way of making sure that they know what is going on in the different sectors of the Treasury as actually to be there and listen to the debate. So I think the co-ordinating role does put a lot of pressure on the organisation.

Here one gets a glimpse of how different the Treasury is from, for example, the Bank of England: a parallel organisation, but one with crucially different pressures and priorities. Anthony Loehnis is in charge of currency markets at the Bank.

Loehnis:

The Treasury are under immediate pressure much of the time, the pressure of parliamentary questions, speeches to be written for debates and all the rest of it. There's a great sense of immediacy. I'm enormously impressed by the amount of work they get through and by the speed with which the Treasury can actually produce a recommendation or view on almost any subject that's put to them, day or night.

A view the Treasury might not dissent from – but evidently it is capable of shame about the amount of paper it consumes.

Middleton:

The Bank actually like to operate like Bankers. They like good verbal communications and to do things by word of mouth. They don't naturally like writing things down, whereas the Treasury does get rid of a lot of trees in the course of its operations, and at times greatly overdoes the amount of paper.[1]

Massive paperwork might seem to betoken a place which put a premium on the orthodox habits of the accomplished draftsman. Not so, apparently:

Priestley:

My experience has been of a number of people that I put very much at the hairy end of the scale. I think in terms of a senior man in the Treasury I met only a few days ago, coming down the Duke of York Steps, eating his lunch out of a paper-bag, for example; or an economist I've had in my

---

1 In the financial year 1982/3 the Central Treasury got through fifty-eight tons of paper (excluding computer print-out).

own office who was a brilliant, unconventional radical; or another economist, with whom I worked some years ago, who was one of the hairiest people I've ever met, but again tremendously able, very much respected by his colleagues. I think it's very much to the credit of the Treasury that it accommodates these people and regards them as a natural part of itself.

And even the ones who opt voluntarily to leave – like Andrew Britton, the new director of the National Institute for Economic and Social Research, and a dissenter from current economic orthodoxies – never quite forget the very special Treasury atmosphere.

Britton:

There is almost an old boys' fellowship. People who have been in the Treasury will tell you that it's a very enjoyable place to work, and although there are rivals, tensions between groups, it's small enough to know everyone. Of course there's also a certain fellow feeling amongst officials as against ministers, and officials as against the general public. It all goes back to the atmosphere of clubbable confidentiality in which the whole system developed in the fifties and sixties, when the Treasury really felt it was running the world.

Its intellectual style is also different from some of the institutions it works with. Nowadays, younger civil servants are sent out much more than they used to be to get experience of the 'real world'. Diana Seammen, a history graduate from Sussex, runs the social security side of the Home Finance Division, and had a spell at Warburgs, the merchant bank.

Seammen:

I think that the Treasury is generally better, as you would expect, at analysing a problem and at organising its thoughts on it into a proper, coherent, logical whole. My impression is that the City does less of this, that it's more instinctive, it tends more to go for the right answer because it feels that it is the right answer, whereas in the Treasury one does have to argue something through and to take into account all the factors. It's a very different kind of world because of the nature of the problems you're dealing with. In the City you are distinctly problem-oriented: there is a deal to be done and there are various ways in which it can be done, but you're working within fairly confined parameters. In the

Treasury none of the problems has a solution, they only have one least bad solution, and you can't be sure that when you've solved the problem you've got the right answer, or indeed that it was an answer at all, because the problems go on. You can never actually say, in the way you can in the City, 'we did the deal and we won'. There are occasions, discreet occasions, in the Treasury when you can say that 'we had this particular view about an expenditure proposal and we think we were right, and ministers argued it out and they came to our view of thinking'. But that doesn't mean that the problem has gone away, it's going to come back later in a different form.

Having begun to put some flesh and blood on the mandarins, we must now take the shine off the palace they are supposed to inhabit: a place, surely, of mahoganied offices, thick pile carpets – their density increasing up the executive ladder – hushed corridors and even (if you listen to some of the public service's more virulent critics on the Conservative back-benches) the odd well-stocked cocktail cabinet. In fact, even by Whitehall's meagre standards the Treasury is a spartan and unlovely place. Most people there work in surroundings devoid of the smallest aesthetic appeal: poky, noisy rooms, with doors constantly slamming in the endless red-linoed passages outside, where the only beverage in sight comes from the ubiquitous tea-trolleys.[1] We can exclusively reveal, in fact, that the total sum reimbursed to Treasury officials for drinks in the office in 1982 was less than £150, a fine advertisement for economy in practice.[2] Compared with many private organisations – not to mention the French Treasury, housed in a wing of the Louvre – the Treasury offers no more pleasing comfort, except central heating, than it did when it was built, in the last century.[3]

---

1 Whilst we were recording the series, the Treasury were examining the case for ending the provision of tea for officers at their desks, but not at meetings. The choice, we were told, was not 'between the existing practice and vending machines, but between the existing practice and leaving people to make their own arrangements'. Six months later, in July 1983, no decision had yet been reached.

2 Assistant Secretaries and above may also entertain visitors (but not other civil servants) outside the Treasury, provided expenditure is kept within the limit of £10 per head.

3 Joan Kelley, now an Under Secretary, told us that when she joined the Treasury in 1954 one of her first duties in the morning was to light the coal fire.

It does, however, have some new inhabitants, none more numerous than economists. And it also has a far more serious attitude to economics itself – the very science and subject the Treasury is supposed to have been dealing with since it began. Everyone there now reckons to be some species of economist. Rachel Lomax is a Senior Economic Adviser and one of the full-time professionals.

Lomax:

The number of economists in the Treasury has increased enormously even since I've been here in the late sixties. There was a big expansion in the early seventies, and a lot of people that were recruited then have aged and moved up the hierarchy, and so, in a sense, they are more obvious further up the departments than they were. The other thing that has happened, at least to my observation, is that the administrators have become economically a good deal more literate.

The growth in the numbers of economists is indeed very striking. In 1964 there were twenty-one of them in the entire government economic service. Now the number is 274, of which sixty-five are in the Treasury – a caste who have quickly taken on both the old Treasury's self-confidence and its clubby working style.

Lomax:

In a sense, we're the higher intellectuals of the building and unselfconsciously preserve an anti-hierarchical, informal working atmosphere.

The effect of this ascendancy is a matter of very considerable debate. But what is indisputable, and the subject of numerous Treasury jokes, is that the immense multiplication of government economists has risen in ominous parallel with the relative decline of the British economy. Sir Douglas Wass sees the rise of the economists as running benignly in line with political demands – and, in making his argument, teaches us that one of the mandarin's necessary skills is the drawing of distinctions. Does the Treasury run economic policy better now that economics has so much higher a priority among top Treasury people?

Wass:

I think I'd slightly quarrel with you over the term 'runs economic policy', but if you will allow me to reformulate that question in terms of 'makes financial economic judgements and analyses, and inferences from statistical data' – I'm sorry to be pedantic, but if I can put in all those terms – no, I think we do those things better now than we would have been able to do them, say, twenty-five, thirty years ago, because we have people who have some familiarity with economic and statistical concepts. But of course I think twenty-five – or perhaps thirty – years ago there wasn't the same volume of data on which those sort of judgements were made. In other words, the requirement for us to be more economically sophisticated matches the requirement of the political scene for politicians to show awareness of these things.

Not every politician who's been in the Treasury seems to accept that things have been quite so desirably arranged. Denis Healey, as everyone knows, is a very clever fellow who, when he was Chancellor from 1974 to 1979, mastered the concepts and language of economics with effortless bravura.

Healey:

I think what is important is to learn what you might call the ABC of the economic situation, and to that extent I think having learnt economics at a university from people who never had to deal with a real decision in their lives may be of some assistance. But I'm not sure the Treasury dealt with the problems of the real world worse when it was staffed entirely by people who had studied Latin and Greek and ancient history and ancient philosophy rather than economics.[1] Economics is not a science: it's a bastard branch of sociology, which is not a science. It assumes that by studying what people did twenty or thirty years ago you can guess what they will do in the next ten years – and that's a very inadequate assumption on which to base a theory.

Nor is such scepticism, it turns out, confined solely to politicians disgruntled by years of man-to-man combat with the public

---

1 In 1982 the Central Treasury graduate recruitment was as follows:

Main Degree Subject	Number of Entrants
Economics	6
Maths/Economics	2
PPE	1
Economics, Accountancy and Financial Management	1
Logic with Maths	1
Environmental Biology	1

sector borrowing requirement. Among officials too, while economists are held to be necessary, there is a strong desire not
to be bamboozled by them. Peter Middleton, now a Deputy
Secretary, is about to take over from Douglas Wass in the top
job[1] having leap-frogged a rank, partly, it is said, because as a
rather hairy non-Oxbridge man (he did economics at Sheffield),
he particularly appeals to Mrs Thatcher's penchant for non-
establishment types. But Middleton's view of economics is close
to Denis Healey's.

Middleton:

I think it would be a dreadful mistake to equate economics
with real life. I think the Treasury is a good deal more in
touch with economic thinking, and I think that is necessary.
But of course there's more to life than being in touch with
economic thinking. First of all, it goes through enormous
gyrations itself, and there is a tendency for economists to
believe the economy is there to be experimented on, which
of course it isn't. Secondly, I think that if one's talking about
real life, the people who are far closer to real life are the
politicians. Indeed, I would say that is their major role in
the department. They meet people all the time; they have
surgeries; they have constituencies; they are actually the
people who have more of a feel for the way the public think,
the way the public act, and especially how they react to
particular things, and what's tolerable and not tolerable,
than any number of economists.

But this is not a depiction which all economists are going to take
lying down. While not wanting to arrogate political decisions to
themselves, there's a sense among government economists that
they are decidedly not back-room boys. They live in the real
world, they think, just as much as the administrators; and,
indeed, these two categories of Treasury persons have almost
been merged. We have it on the authority of none other than
the Chief Economic Adviser.

Burns:

In the Treasury there is a very close relationship between
the economists and the administrators. There is not a clear
dividing line between the economist working away in the
dungeon at his numbers and the administrators who are
involved in all the issues relating to politics. The economists

---

1 He became Permanent Secretary on 1 April 1983.

are very closely involved in all of the policy decisions. Of course we have a number of people who started life as economists who are now administrators,[1] and a number of economists who do administrative jobs from time to time. We have a group who work very closely with people in the overseas finance area. We have other people who work closely with those who are involved in organising the budgetary work. But I think the major characteristics, if one wanted to try and distinguish them, is that the economists are overwhelmingly dealing with what would be described as the analytical background and with the quantification of that. The administrators are dealing with the whole question of getting a policy discussed, getting it in place, and then making it operational. But they really work quite closely together, it's not the back-room relationship which very often typifies specialists in organisations.

Andrew Britton, on the other hand, seems to be arguing for more respect for the academic discipline in all its purity. He delineates the two pitfalls – of excessive power and excessive propaganda – into which Treasury economists can all too easily be lured by the seduction of politics.

Britton:

What is the role of the Treasury economist? There are two possible models for this, neither of which corresponds exactly to reality or necessarily works very well. One is that the Treasury economist is somehow acting as an arbiter in the debate over policy. There have been attempts by, for example, the Parliamentary Select Committee,[2] to bring in the Treasury economists as expert witnesses against their own ministers. Nothing could be more objective than this role. Treasury economists might even find it congenial in some ways. But from the point of view of the smooth running of life within the Treasury and, indeed, the constitutional position of ministerial responsibility for the working of the Treasury, one cannot have a body within a department of state which is acting as arbiter over its own ministers, at least in public. And therefore I think that that superficially

---

1 Rachel Lomax, a Senior Economic Adviser who contributed to the series (*see* p. 18), moved, two months after we recorded the interview with her, to an administrative post concerned with monetary policy.
2 The Select Committee on the Treasury and Civil Service.

attractive model for the Treasury economic service actually comes up against some fairly fundamental problems. The alternative pole, the opposite pole to this, would be the position in which the Treasury economists really became apologists for the views of the government of the day. Now that would be at least as uncongenial, if that were to be the role. One would in fact have to see a great deal more changeover of staffs within the government's economic service when governments changed. But a public presentation, a public role, for Treasury economists must tend always to veer either in one direction or the other – either to being apologists for the government or standing in judgement on the government. I think neither is tenable, and that the best role for a government economist, therefore, is essentially a quiet one. They shouldn't appear a lot in public. There are lots of economists in a position outside government to comment in public, to keep the public informed, aware of what the government is doing and the arguments for and against, and I think the public debate is better conducted between them.

This professional modesty derives, in part, from a deeper point, about history. Twenty years ago, when the place was not nearly so full of economists, it also had a much clearer and more assured view of its own essential rightness than it does today. It really thought it ran the world – and knew how the world worked. David Hancock, a Treasury man now in the Cabinet Office, and about to take over before he's fifty as Permanent Secretary at the Education ministry, once thought the economy could indeed be fine-tuned from Whitehall.

Hancock:

In the days of my youth we used to think we could manage the British economy within very precise guidelines. We worked out the expected pressures and demand on output, and it either fell below or it fell above, and we adjusted taxation accordingly and we expected it all to come out perfectly. We had no adverse effects on the exchange rate or the rate of inflation or anything else. We don't think in those terms any more, we're much more realistic about what the effects of government actions are. It's not only true of this country, it's true throughout the western world.

Few in number though economists were, in the old days they expressed a consensus, which Geoff Littler, now the Second

Permanent Secretary in charge of overseas finance, depicts as an intellectual monolith.

Littler:

Outsiders like myself – I was not trained as an economist – and those who were in those days at the top of the Treasury were induced to believe the consensus among economists, and in the absence of respectable argument to the contrary, to assume that what they indicated was the right basis for policy, and the only problem was 'could you do it?'

Now, however, diversity is all – or would 'naked uncertainty' better describe it?

Littler:

If you look around now, it is true that there are more professionally trained economists in the Treasury, and more people, either professionally trained or very substantially experienced, at the top of the Treasury who are sufficiently experienced to discuss economic arguments with good intelligence among groups of economists. The striking feature is the very considerable range of economic philosophies, and the differences in those philosophies are certainly reflected in this building. So that if you think of the diffident non-professional looking at the range of economic advice he may get, he is less inclined to rely totally on what he may be told by anyone, he's less inclined to believe that whatever he's told and accepts is bound to be right. Consequently, there is a good deal more difficulty for us all in reaching judgements of what we ought to be doing, let alone what we can actually do.

And can a political lead cut through their difficulties?

Littler:

That helps enormously. We are, after all, the servants of the political masters of the day, and if they give us a strong lead, the fact that there is no solid body of received doctrine which is in conflict with that lead makes it that much easier for us all to accept it and fit in with it. This leaves people who have dissenting views in a slightly uncomfortable position, but I think, on the whole, if the lead is strong enough, those dissenting views are positively welcomed, because they're assisting general understanding of why we're doing something which is different or in that particular form, and they make sure that we have actually looked at the other side of things as well.

This theory was put to the test, with a vengeance, in May 1979, when a government arrived in power seemingly afflicted by no intellectual doubts whatever. Although this account will be dominated by the voices of officials – and is decidedly not an exploration of economic policy – it's impossible to remove the Treasury from its political context. One assumption widely made and discussed after Mrs Thatcher's arrival in power, with her extreme monetarist views and her determination to make economic policy cleave to a handful of inflexible targets, was that the inhabitants of the Treasury did not like it – that they simply disagreed with a government bent on dismantling the orthodoxies inherited from John Maynard Keynes. Let's hope we've already shown that the consensus about such orthodoxies was already breaking down. We put to Douglas Wass the hypothesis that, in this situation, it must be helpful to have a government which is so certain about what should be done.

Wass:

Is there such a government? I don't know that there is. I assume you are referring to the present administration, but I think that there is plenty of evidence from ministerial speeches to show that there is at least a certain amount of uncertainty about what is the right course in any particular circumstances. Of course, every government will present its policy prescriptions, when it presents them to Parliament, as the right ones. In a sense, this is the way politics work – it's a thesis and an antithesis put out by the Opposition. Policy is not presented in a highly speculative, philosophical, self-doubting way, and I think this government is no different from any other government in presenting its policies to the public and to Parliament.

Even officials who have left the Treasury, partly at least because they aren't wholly sympathetic to present policies, characterise the culture-shock of Thatcherism as not so much about substance as style.

Britton:

There was the change in style, which of course goes beyond the Treasury – a feeling that ministers were unsympathetic to the process of administration, unsympathetic to the job which the civil service was trying to do. I think that this had an unnecessarily damaging effect on morale. The Treasury, in particular, had to cope with some rather outspoken criticism of Treasury traditions coming from within its own body, and some individual civil servants may have taken this to heart. But they're a resilient lot and full of this, perhaps unjustified, self-confidence which enables them to ride out the storm.

It could have been a conflict-ridden experience from the other side as well. After all, the Tories had developed certain views about economic policy which inevitably challenged what they saw as the entrenched wisdom of the mandarins. Peter Cropper, from the City and the Conservative Research Department, arrived as one of the new Chancellor's political advisers. But, according to him too – is he being very British and discreet about it? – everything went swimmingly.

Cropper:
I didn't feel that on arrival one was confronting a collection of officials who were deeply committed, almost irrevocably committed, to some set of policies which we were challenging. They had after all seen us coming for some time. There had been a period of six months, a year, some might say longer than that, when it looked pretty inevitable that a Conservative government would succeed that of Mr Callaghan. And we hadn't exactly been secretive about our policy processes. I wasn't conscious of being a member of a small invading force which had to put down the tribes that we found around us. I think it went very smoothly so far as I could judge, and good personal relations seemed to be established between ministers and civil servants very quickly.

But it is the case that civil servants as a breed are different from politicians in at least one crucial psychological respect, which bears on the picture of a smooth Treasury bureaucracy being violated by rude and headstrong Tory ideologues. One of their men in the British Embassy in Washington, economic counsellor Harry Walsh, puts it with the crisp detachment one might expect from a Canadian who has somehow managed to smuggle himself into the higher reaches of the British civil service.

Walsh:
One thing that is characteristic of the British Treasury at the top is that there are no people who are absolute enthusiasts – and by an enthusiast I mean someone who's so dedicated to one set of ideas that he's blinkered to other sets of ideas. Now it seems to me that if you are going to have a permanent civil service, an enthusiast is exactly the last type of

person you would want, because the persons operating the policy have to be able to adapt their ideas to the new lot of ministers coming in.

The Thatcher ministers, however much they learned to love the Treasury, certainly did feel the need for some privacy in developing their ideas. Even in the best-run administrations, according to Peter Cropper, the political collective needs to find ways of keeping itself together.

Cropper:

One really had a double role: part of the time I was reading the official papers as they passed simultaneously across the Chancellor's desk and my own; and then he also made use of our presence at his morning meetings. These meetings were attended by the ministers together with the Special Advisers.[1] The Chancellor used to come in each morning with a bundle of papers arising out of his overnight boxes, and he would like to check his own reactions and opinions against those of the other ministers and the Special Advisers.

Was the absence of civil servants a reflection of the new government's fear that its impulses would be eroded by conventional Treasury wisdom?

Cropper:

That was certainly not the open intention, and I don't even think it was the unconscious intention. The purpose really was to give the Chancellor and the other ministers a chance to let their hair down a bit, to talk informally around difficult subjects, in a way which wouldn't be passed on. It wasn't so much a desire for secrecy, it was a desire to have somewhere where one could experiment a bit, bat ideas around without feeling that people were actually taking every word as being the ministerial observation or comment on a situation. In their busy lives, and I think that their lives are far too busy, they never had time perhaps to prop up the bar in the evening or to go out to lunch round the corner and have a chat, and so there were almost literally no occasions, except for these morning meetings, when the five ministers got together.[2] The presence of the Special Advisers was in a

1 The Treasury Ministers' Special Advisers during the Conservative Administration of 1979–83 were:

   Adam Ridley 1979–   George Cardona 1979–81   Peter Cropper 1979–82
   Robin Harris 1981–3   Douglas French 1982–3

2 In the period when Peter Cropper was a Special Adviser (October 1979–

sense accidental to that, although we did sometimes chip in, we were sometimes invited to express our opinion, and we were also deemed to have read the papers and therefore to be fit to be asked one or two questions. I think it was helpful for the Chancellor, who, after all, had known us as people for about five years, to have around him some people who had grown into his way of looking at things, who had shared common past experiences, who could share a few in-jokes and who could laugh about colleagues just occasionally in a friendly sort of way. It was really all a matter of the Chancellor being able to try out an idea or a reaction on us, and being either encouraged or discouraged if we came out with the same answer as he did.

According to the Chancellor himself, it was a process which bore fruit. His ideas – the ideas of the politician – acquired a resonance with the department. Sir Geoffrey is a convert and so, he insists, are his officials – no longer merely loyal servants but people who, like himself, have seen the light and are now body, soul and mind behind him.

Howe:

Some of the people in the Treasury, the senior people whom I met when I arrived there, had been with me as key officials when I was administering the prices and incomes policy of the Heath government. Ironically enough, when we went to the summit with President Mitterrand[1] I found, as I looked around the room when I was talking to the French Prime Minister, that every single one of the ministers and senior officials present had been directly involved in the introduction and implementation of our prices and incomes policy,[2] and I observed that one of the first things we had done on coming into office was to abolish all those things, and we've now achieved a massive success against price inflation. That

February 1982) the five Treasury Ministers were: the Chancellor, Sir Geoffrey Howe; the Chief Secretary, John Biffen until 5.1.81, then Leon Brittan; the Financial Secretary, Nigel Lawson until 4.9.81, then Nicholas Ridley; the Economic Secretary, Peter Rees until 15.9.81, then Jock Bruce-Gardyne; and the Minister of State, Lord Cockfield. When the Treasury took over the Civil Service Department in November 1981 they were joined by Barney Hayhoe, Minister of State (Civil Service).

1 The eighth world economic summit, hosted by President Mitterrand, was held at Versailles, 4–6 June 1982.

2 They were: Patrick Jenkin, as Secretary of State for Industry, who was Chief Secretary to the Treasury 1970–4 and much engaged in incomes policy problems; Lord Cockfield, as Secretary of State for Trade, who was Chairman of the Price

experience is shared by officials. Many of the things that are common placebos and prescriptions have been tried by them as well as us. And I sense a feeling of respect, and adventure if you like, in sharing the intellectual, practical challenge of putting the right policies in place and having the courage to sustain them.

Eloquent support for this view of the Treasury as a *learning* institution comes from the opposite political quarter. Michael Posner was an economic adviser to numerous Labour ministers from 1964 onwards. He sees the place united in at least one objective: its recognition, and exercise, of power.

Posner:

The Treasury is a powerful machine. It's there to serve ministers and has a free discussion system between officials and ministers which has no parallel that I've seen in any other government department. Ministers and officials argue with each other fairly continually, and they influence each other. And through the fire of controversy and, even more important, through the fire of experience, they get welded together as a new metal. That happened, I'm sure, in 1964 when that Labour government came in, it happened under Mr Healey who had many monetarist notions, and I've no doubt that it happened again under Sir Geoffrey Howe. The Treasury always like to feel that the policy which it's following is the right and correct policy. In a sense TINA, 'there is no alternative', should be written over the portals of the Treasury. They really do believe that the policy they're pursuing is the right policy, and it's natural for officials and ministers to hold that what they're doing is unquestionably correct, and very often it is. So I'm sure that when the Conservative government first came in in 1979, there was initial disarray and argument and controversy and contradiction of the old ways of doing things. I'm sure that what then happened was that they came together and that that coming together is naturally cemented by the process of promotion and retirement of officials. As the ministerial team stays and gets stronger and more decided in its views, then officials

---

Commission 1973–7; Ken Couzens, then Treasury Second Permanent Secretary in charge of overseas finance and from 1973–7 Treasury Deputy Secretary in charge of prices and incomes policy; and Robin Gray, Deputy Secretary in the Department of Trade now, and around 1973 Under Secretary in charge of prices policy in that Department.

begin to accommodate themselves to the dominant view, not through any slavish adherence to the doctrine of the day, but because officials do exist to carry out government policy.

TINA, however, is a creation which makes Douglas Wass shudder. No such notion, he insists, could ever grip the constantly probing mind of Treasury Man.

Wass:

I'm surprised that Michael Posner, who, after all, worked here, should say that, because he's been party to many discussions that have taken place round this table, and indeed elsewhere in the Treasury, where there's been a good deal of debate as to whether the policy being pursued was uniquely right or whether some change was required. No, I think if the Treasury appears to be confident that the policy it's following is uniquely right, it's really doing no more than the apologist of any policy would do when he's defending it. We want to argue the case for the policy that is being followed by ministers, just as any other department would, in the best possible light. But when it comes to internal discussion, of course, we're always discussing the possibility of a change of policy, although for the most part potential change is discussed in marginal terms and not in revolutionary terms. It would be rare for any department to wake up one morning and say to itself 'We've been following the completely wrong policy, let us about turn and do something quite different'. If, at any time, that were to arise, it would arise in a very evolutionary way. There would be a gradual perception that things weren't happening as it was expected or hoped that they would happen. We would look at why that had happened, discussing it as an ongoing business among ourselves and with ministers, and there would be a gradual evolution towards perhaps some changes, perhaps tightening up the policy, perhaps relaxation of policy. If the situation was getting wildly out of hand there might even have to be a radical change in policy. So I don't think there is any disposition within the Treasury for saying any policy is uniquely right and must not be changed. That's a quite wrong description.

Those who see Treasury officials, in harmony or not, as a rival power centre to their ministers seem to be travelling fast down a cul-de-sac. Certainly the official Treasury is powerful. It has access to the Chancellor. It influences his options. And being a small body of men and women, who get to know each other well, it grants this access and occasional influence to young as well as old. But far from being secretly dominated by officials, the Treasury is the most political of all departments, and if its ministers are worth their salt, there's little which happens there that they don't know about. The danger, in fact, may be almost the opposite. As Diana Seammen suggests, they can be so sensitive to their masters' needs as to be even more political than the politicians.

Seammen:

People in the Treasury are highly politically aware. Sometimes, you can argue, perhaps a bit too politically aware. It's amusing to see civil servants putting up minutes to politicians pointing out all the political difficulties that might arise. And the ministers sometimes say, 'Oh well, you know we can wear this'. The fashion is to say that civil servants are not sufficiently politicised, but I think that sometimes you can argue they're too much so. The Treasury, in particular, has to be a very political department, because anything it deals with has huge political sensitivities.

A different perspective on the sources of Treasury power can be gained by looking at its relations outside. It bestrides Whitehall, yet, as David Hancock says, it acquires a major part of its identity and *esprit de corps* from the assaults constantly being made upon it.

Hancock:

I think it's the sort of collegiate atmosphere that you get in an institution which is constantly embattled. The Treasury has its objectives to pursue, which are different from those of other departments. I mean, a system of financial control in any institution is essentially one of tension, and the effect of that on the people inside is rather like that of people in a siege; it develops a sort of fellow-feeling, and self-confidence comes from that, I think.

Whether this adds up to a consciousness of power is, as usual, much evaded. There's always a great deal of self-deprecation among British civil servants, even ones as senior as Douglas Wass who may look as though they sit at the centre of the centre of decision-making.

Wass:

I don't think that I live my life like that, and I don't think

41

people who may be at the centre of the centre of things do. I think you keep your sanity by saying, 'Well, here's a job to be done, here are some papers to be dealt with', and you deal with them as best you can, and you put on your hat and coat at the end of the day and you go home and you live like a normal human being. And I don't think you really sort of strike your head and say, 'Gosh, you know, 300,000 people are going to be better off next week as a result of a decision the Chancellor took on my recommendation last night'. I don't think you look at it in those sort of dramatic and human terms all the time. Of course, in dealing with a problem which may affect a lot of people, you're never unmindful of the impact of this on people. But that isn't the emotional environment in which you operate – I think you tend to be much more clinical and objective, 'Here is a problem, what is the best way to deal with it? Here is a solution I think is right.'

So to talk about the Treasury being a centre of power was much too crude a statement?

Wass:

Much too crude a statement.

Nevertheless millions of people can be affected by the Treasury's actions, and in the words of Peter Middleton, who will succeed Wass in April, one catches the equally authentic voice of what one must still feel free to call a 'Treasury Mandarin', even though we've tried to redefine his character. Middleton shows that the old self-confidence, not to mention the old desire for control, is not entirely dead.

Middleton:

I think the Treasury works better when it's got a small organisation which is moderately overworked, if I could put it that way. It is a question of style, but I think the ideal organisation for the Treasury would be one in which everybody was free to take their own decisions – and we told them which decisions to take.

What he was particularly talking about was public spending, when the Treasury does constant battle with the rest of Whitehall. But that last line, with its whiff of wishful arrogance, will stand as a motif of the Treasury mind. Nowadays it may be less sure of itself, and bestride Whitehall and the world far less mightily than it once did. But that does not mean to say it would not like to.

The Language of Priorities

First Broadcast: 6 March 1983

Monetarists may come and Keynesians may go, but public spending goes on for ever. No matter what economic theories now prevail, or what government is in power, the control of public expenditure remains the Treasury's unalterable function. Governments everywhere, from the most primitive to the most sophisticated, need something resembling a ministry of finance, to keep their extravagant plans in fleeting contact with the straight and narrow.

Huge controversy has from time to time attended the British Treasury's attitudes to spending. 'Meanness', 'penny-pinching' and 'incessant interference' are some of the politer descriptions of its customary behaviour. But to insiders the job is more like a sacred trust, calling on the eternal vigilance of an élite corps of dedicated public servants. Joan Kelley is one of them: she joined the civil service in 1949 and is now the Under Secretary in charge of the Treasury's HE group, which includes the Home Office, Education and Transport. All that spending comes under her.

Kelley:
What I say to staff who come new to my group is that there are really about 250 people on the public expenditure side of the Treasury, and they are surrogates for the thirty million taxpayers. Their objective is not to get immersed too much in the merits of any particular policy, but first to look at whether what is being proposed is compatible with the department's agreed public expenditure programme and with the policy of the government as a whole on these matters. So you should be thinking here in rather puritanical terms about the burden on the taxpayer, and it is really quite salutary sometimes to say to a spending department, which is trying to persuade you to accept a case in principle for something, 'Do you consider that this can be justified if we have to add one penny in the pound on the standard rate?' It is remarkable how people close their minds to this sort of thing. Often it comes as a great shock to them to be asked to consider it in these terms, which is why I say you always have to push the argument back into a question of priorities.

Ultimately that argument is settled, of course, by politicians, and we'll come back to them later. But the truth is that the mere mention of ministers does not – as the stuffier civil servants sometimes imply – end all description of the Treasury's role. Where to place the emphasis of this role varies, not surprisingly, from official to official. Joan Kelley's boss is Sir Anthony Rawlinson, the Second Permanent Secretary in charge of public spending.[1] He puts most emphasis on making the big sums add up.

Rawlinson:

The role of the Treasury is primarily, though not exclusively, concerned with the aggregate of public spending, with the aggregate of the various programmes that make up the whole, and their influence on the economy in the light of the government's current economic strategy. Value for money is a very important element as well, but it stands alongside the overall objective of managing the total.

Down at a lower level there also seems to be this reluctance to admit to anything like interference in the details of spending. Stephen Godber is the Principal in charge of spending on housing.[2]

Godber:

I don't think the Treasury necessarily has a housing policy. It will have a housing aspect of a general public expenditure policy, and if there are general policy objectives, such as keeping the level of public expenditure down or trying to shift the balance between capital and current expenditure, then that will influence the attitude that one takes to policy issues that come up in housing. But I don't think it has a free-standing housing policy as such.

Where details matter is when they bear on value for money – which is rather less grand than 'policy', but is at the heart of the Treasury's *raison d'être*. Nick Sallnow-Smith,[3] the Principal in charge of higher education spending, was rather inclined to scoff – as Treasury men are sometimes wont to – at the suggestion that his main job was simply to say 'No' to the excessive demands of the spenders:

---

1 Sir Anthony Rawlinson became Permanent Secretary at the Department of Trade on 28 April 1983. He was replaced by Alan Bailey (*see* p. 18).

2 Stephen Godber completed his secondment to the Treasury from the DHSS in March 1983.

3 Nick Sallnow-Smith left the Treasury for a two-year secondment to Manufacturers' Hanover Trust, the bankers, in February 1983.

Sallnow-Smith:

That is the usual caricature, and like all caricatures there is an element of truth to it, but the relationship has much more to it than that. For a start, it implies that the Treasury is only interested in the totals, and indeed some people believe that that is true. I don't think it is, because we also have a role in trying to achieve value for money, and in encouraging departments to look for that. Now that can be done at the level of the systems that one tries to operate, systems of cash limits and cash planning, and also at the level of considering with departments particular policy proposals on which we will subsequently advise our respective ministers. We're interested not only in whether it costs x million pounds, but what that x million pounds is intended to do, and you can't have a sensible discussion about a proposal unless you do that.

Another popular caricature casts the Treasury in the role of scapegoat. Diana Seammen is an Assistant Secretary in charge of monitoring spending on social security.

Seammen:

There's a disposition to think that every spending decision is one that's taken by the Treasury, particularly of course if it's an unpopular one. I suppose departments play that game a bit as well, they say to clients, 'Sorry, it wasn't us, it was the Treasury'. But the fact is that departmental ministers make their own decisions about spending, and although the Treasury will normally vet those decisions and approve them, nonetheless it's essentially a department's business to control its own spending. This idea that the Treasury is all-powerful and all-seeing is really quite pervasive. I think MPs and politicians of all hues share this feeling, and they'll always want to put down questions that have got anything to do with expenditure for the Treasury, in the belief that we know it all.

The spending departments, naturally, are only too keen to confirm that they are their own best monitors. Was it wrong, we asked the Permanent Secretary at the DHSS, Sir Kenneth Stowe, to see the Treasury as the one true exponent of cost control?

Stowe:

Quite wrong. We have a very strong finance control system in a big organisation like the DHSS. The Principal Finance

Officer is one of the key Deputy Secretaries. He has an essential role to play, as do his division, in the development of policies, in the assessment of priorities, and in control of the use of resources. His division ought to be – and I believe it is – a very powerful presence throughout the whole of the administration of the department.

The nature of the relationship between spenders and providers is what our discussion is mainly about. And it is, in fact, not at all straightforward. The Treasury has the money, but does it really have the knowledge? How can its tiny body of officials do battle on even terms with the massed ranks of departmental special interests? Take one of the biggest spenders of all – the Ministry of Defence – now responsible for a £14,000 million annual budget. The Treasury Permanent Secretary, Sir Douglas Wass, says he has his own defence experts on tap.

Wass:

In our defence expenditure division we do have people who are making a continuing study of defence expenditure, of defence strategy, defence options, defence policy and all that. And as a result of their direct experience with the Ministry of Defence, and by studying the problem them-selves, they are very sophisticated people who know a good deal about defence strategy and defence options. If they thought that the Ministry of Defence were – and this is a very unlikely proposition – seeking to spend money uneco-nomically on buying some particular weaponry that was inef-ficient, they would certainly say so.

They reckon they can argue about weaponry systems on equal terms.

Wass:

A weapon system of British origin might be preferred by the Chiefs of Staff, perhaps because buying British gave greater security of supply in times of different international tension or whatever. But our Defence people might claim to know that there was an equivalent system – perhaps available in the United States – at lesser cost and there would then be an argument as to whether the premium being paid for security of supply was worthwhile. But we would seek to set up the argument between ourselves and the Ministry of Defence; if we didn't have that capability we would never be able to challenge the totality of defence expenditure.

But there's a problem here. Where does the Treasury get this capability? Primarily from one source. Desmond Bryars is Principal Finance Officer at the Ministry of Defence, and as he says, knowledge is power.

Bryars:

Everybody's judgement is coloured by what they know, and it is quite true that what they know is what they learn from us. Now, what they learn from us is not necessarily what we tell them, because they're in a position to ask intelligent questions. They occupy a central position, have contact with all parts of the department, and they will know what the left hand in the Ministry of Defence is doing, as well as what the right hand is doing, and they can put two and two together. They are in a position to ask intelligent questions and they do ask intelligent questions.

This sounds a bit different from Douglas Wass's argument between equals about weapons systems. Even more diminishing is the version according to Sir Frank Cooper who, until Christmas 1982, was the Permanent Secretary at Defence, sitting opposite Sir Douglas at the apex of the dialogue.

Cooper:

I think the Treasury is rather sensible about this. Quite a long time ago they gave up the idea that they knew very much about weaponry, and there's no way the people in DM, which is the division of the Treasury which deals with the Ministry of Defence, could possibly come to a clean verdict about a particular weapon system.

Make no mistake, however, the argument about money is still very real.

Cooper:

What happens in government and within the Cabinet is this: that you get a very large measure of agreement between the bureaucracy on how about 98-point-something per cent of the money, that is available to the country as a whole, is going to be spent. You are then on the margins. Now they're big margins. The arguments between the Ministry of Defence and the Treasury are not about x billion pounds at all; they're arguments about two or three hundred million pounds, and it's a test of manliness, I suppose, as to who's the strongest, who's going to last out the longest. There's an element of that in it, that's certainly true.

Occasionally these margins can be so narrow as to reach the outer limits of self-parody.

Cooper:

I suppose the other area is the extent to which they mess about – and I use those words advisedly – with trivia. And they do mess about with trivia on the personnel side, on the miscellaneous side. There's a true story in the Ministry of Defence that two Deputy Secretaries some ten or more years ago had a tremendous argument as to whether the Ministry of Defence could buy a television set, about which two Deputy Secretaries wrote long letters to each other for months.

So vast is the expenditure already spoken for and unalterable, in fact, that there's a sense in which any contest *can* only exist at the margin – although perhaps not quite so close to its outer edge as that. Speaking of the DHSS budget, Diana Seammen is quite clear about that – and also about the moment at which the ministers take over from the bureaucrats.

Seammen:

If the whole £34,000 million were subject to decisions every day, one clearly couldn't cope. A lot of it is bespoke – the statutes lay down who is entitled to what and at what rates they're entitled to it – so one is operating very much at the margin.[1] Still, there are decisions to be taken at the margin as you go along and of course there's always room for constant improvement, pressure for improvements on social security, new benefits, extending eligibility for existing benefits for other people. Then every year there are the bread-and-butter issues of uprating those benefits by how much, and on the side of revenue-raising there's the National Insurance contributions review which happens in the autumn of each year and gets announced in November or early December. The extent of the influence that you can have over this as an Assistant Secretary in the Treasury is rather limited. Again, it's the nature of the decisions; they all involve large amounts of money – there's very rarely anything I do that

---

1 On 7 July 1983 Sir Geoffrey Howe's successor as Chancellor, Nigel Lawson, announced an emergency package of £500 million expenditure cuts, because 'it is now clear that public expenditure is running at a significantly higher level than is consistent with the 1983-4 planning total of £119.6 billion'. (*Official Report*, HC Vol. 45, no. 16, 7 July 1983, col. 418–429). Norman Fowler, Secretary of State for Social Services, said (*The Times*, 8 July 1983) that DHSS programmes were running at £300 million more than planned, two-thirds of which was from social security spending, i.e. the 'bespoken' part of his budget, which was affected not by cash limits but by the take-up rate of fixed benefits.

I feel I shouldn't actually submit to Treasury ministers, usually the Chief Secretary for his approval, because anything involves millions.

Moreover, she is quite candid about the limits of what any Treasury official can even know.

Seammen:

In my job there are ten of us altogether – that's including clerical support – dealing with the entire spending on the staff and benefit side of the Department of Health and Social Security. Now it stands to reason that there's quite a lot of what the department does that we don't actually see and we don't know about. Overall the system should ensure that public expenditure is planned according to faintly rational principles – whether it does, that's another matter, that's what it's designed to do. But there are quite large areas of departmental spending on which the Treasury is not expert, cannot by nature of what it is and how many we are, be expert on everything that's done. I think it's amazing that we are expert, in the superficial sense that we are, on all the main areas.

The spenders admit that expert knowledge gives them power, but not absolute power: whether they are the Permanent Secretary,

Stowe:

Yes, we control the knowledge, but rightly we have to satisfy the Treasury that we are using our knowledge and our resources in a way that is consistent with the central policies of the government of the day.

Or the Department's Principal Finance Officer, Geoffrey Hulme,

Hulme:

In a way one is necessarily selecting information. It's an enormously complex field and clearly in presenting our case one selects, but I would have said that we, and indeed other departments, attempt to play this straight with the Treasury, just as we would expect them to play it straight with us. We would not make statements that could not be fully substantiated or that were not in fact fair statements or reasonable judgements of the case. I mean clearly these are matters of judgement; we are presenting a case and in a sense one is in a position perhaps of the advocate, but we are not wanting, as it were, to mislead the court.

And in the end, the Treasury is very much aware that this is its role, as the next most important arbiter before the ultimate court of appeal, the Cabinet itself. Douglas Wass returns to his example from the Ministry of Defence.

Wass:

I think if we're really persuaded that within the framework of government policy and the government's financial economic objectives a particular course was right – I mean, take, for instance, the one I just gave you, of a particular weapon system being as effective, but very much cheaper, from one source or another – then certainly we would argue very strongly. Just how strongly would depend on the degree of conviction we had that the premium being paid for security of supply wasn't excessive. If it was marginal, we might put the point to the Ministry of Defence, discuss it with them, and then at the end of the day they'll either accept our point of view or perhaps we would accept theirs. It depends entirely on how convinced we are by our own arguments.

You don't have to be a politician to have convictions.

Nor are Treasury people the only ones who have them. Frank Cooper, for one, makes that clear enough. On the other hand, one can overdo the picture of Whitehall as a battlefield. At one level the departments see each other as rivals. But at another the senior professional bureaucrat may see it as a point of honour to believe that he is engaged in the united task of keeping the show on the road. Sir Kenneth Stowe, Permanent Secretary of the department Diana Seammen is invigilating, doesn't see the Treasury and DHSS as even having different interests.

Stowe:

Far from it being an adversarial relationship, I see it as a continuing, constructive dialogue. It's not by any means a mutual admiration society; they sometimes think we're potty, and sometimes we think they may not have it quite the right way round, and I don't think either of us would feel inhibited from saying so. But it is, nevertheless, a relationship which is founded, I believe, on a mutual awareness of the fact that the government is a seamless robe, and that in a department as big as the DHSS with enormous operational responsibilities, you have got to keep continuously in the forefront of your mind that the department exists to do the business for which it was set up. The

Treasury is as well aware of that as we are.

In the Treasury they seem to take a slightly more fighting view – but they're also aware of politics. Diana Seammen puts a gloss on the notion that departments make 'bids', of which it's the Treasury official's job invariably to take the sternest possible view.

Seammen:

Yes, I think that's the job. Yes, one's negotiating. You're conscious of the political pressures on your spending department, you know that their ministers have got to get up and defend it, but you can't separate that from the government as a whole. If their ministers get into bad political trouble, the government as a whole is probably heading for trouble, particularly on something as sensitive as social security. So it's not just a question of saying 'no' and sticking to it, even if one could. There wouldn't actually be much of a job if that was all you had to do.

And Sir Kenneth would be horrified at any suggestion that his department might be at all selective in what it told the Treasury.

Stowe:

I don't recognise that at all, that simply is not consistent with the actuality of our relationship. If I thought that any of my staff here were suppressing or editing information passing between this department and the Treasury, I would be very angry about it, because it wouldn't in the long run be in the interest of the department. Certainly it wouldn't be in the interest of this department's ministers, nor of the many different clientele whom we exist to serve, because sooner or later something would go wrong, as a result of having only a partial awareness in the Treasury of what it is that we're doing.

It is, in fact, only with the politicians that one begins to get a taste of what some of these conflicts mean in human terms. Presiding over the whole public spending process is the Chief Secretary at the Treasury, Leon Brittan.[1] We put to Brittan that Whitehall was itself a political community, characterised by intensely competitive power centres, with the Treasury portrayed as the villain of the piece.

---

1 After the General Election on 9 June 1983 Leon Brittan became Home Secretary and was succeeded as Chief Secretary by Peter Rees.

Brittan:

I don't think there's a substantial disagreement about the facts, I don't think that anything you've said about the system would be disputed by anyone – it's the adjectives and adverbs that there may be disagreement about. Now whether you regard these discussions and the sort of way they're resolved as being most appropriately described in the highly coloured language of the jungle, or whether you regard it as being a civilised way of deciding on public business, is a matter of taste. I suspect it sometimes more resembles the one and sometimes more resembles the other.

Moreover, in this dialogue, the balance of responsibility has shifted. Sir Anthony Rawlinson has seen many ebbs and flows.

Rawlinson:

Over the last, shall we say, twenty-five years or more there has been a very decided swing towards greater delegation to departments and disengagement of the Treasury from the detail of expenditure. At the moment, partly because of the present government's concern with systems of management in departments and a desire that the Treasury should exercise some leadership in this area, the pendulum is swinging a little the other way. But we do in principle try to delegate authority for the detail of spending to departments, subject to some views about the competence of the department to handle the detail, and also subject to the need for the Treasury to keep itself sufficiently informed about what is happening in a department to be able to exercise an intelligent role in the fields that are proper to it.

Altogether, the power of relatively junior Treasury officials to call the shots seems to have been much modified. People like David Hancock, a Treasury man in the Cabinet Office, regard it as very old hat.

Hancock:

I think that's rather an old-fashioned view of Treasury control, frankly. The big matters which the Treasury gets involved in, that is to say, the assessment of particular projects, go to ministers, and the Treasury is involved because it has to brief the Chancellor for the ministerial discussion. Smaller projects aren't vetted now by the Treasury in the way they used to be, so you don't have a very young man telling a responsible Finance Officer that he's got it all wrong and he shouldn't be building a by-pass round Stevenage, or whatever. It doesn't happen like that anymore. In the old days, to some extent it did. When I joined the Treasury there was an element of that, but it was already dying fast.

Not that by-passes have entirely lost their charm for the Treasury. Joan Kelley is the Under Secretary in charge of them.

Kelley:

This is a big running programme and the arrangement we have with the Department of Transport is that they have an accepted cost-benefit technique for evaluating the value of new roads. We satisfy ourselves on the technique, and then, on the whole, the only projects which we see are those which do not meet accepted tests of value, but where for one reason or another the department wishes to go ahead with a road even though it does not meet the criteria. For example, you could have a situation where the by-pass was being proposed to a standard which was greater than the traffic or other demands might suggest. It could be higher than the norm because extra attention was being paid to the landscaping or the gradient or the access roads – matters like that. The discussion would be largely on things like standards and costs. There are three people who deal with the road programme and evaluate the other Department of Transport stuff, such as the total of the proposals for road capital and maintenance in the course of the public expenditure survey.

According to Sir Anthony, this has given rise to problems about job-satisfaction.

Rawlinson:

Rather fewer decisions are taken in the Treasury at a low level, because things that can be decided at that level are not normally referred to the Treasury. This has in fact created a certain managerial problem in the Treasury, in that there is much less to be decided by the junior ranks than there was a generation ago.[1]

When such decisions *are* made by junior people, however, they seem to meet with approval.

Brittan:

I have yet to find an example of a consent that has been given by a civil servant which I regard as being objectionable,

---

1 *See* p. 18.

either on the grounds that the amount of money in relation to the programme is such that it ought to have been referred to me, even if I would have readily agreed with it, or on the grounds that the quality and the type and the novelty of the expenditure raise issues which I would wish to consider myself. I haven't found that this is a serious problem at all.

This question of levels of discretion has another aspect. Is there a figure above which departments are obliged to seek Treasury consent: and below which they are free to do what they want? Geoffrey Hulme, at the DHSS, gave one clear answer.

Hulme:

Schemes over £10 million do require Treasury approval at the first stage. There are a number of stages in building a hospital: you decide the plan, you approve the scheme in principle as to whether it fits into the plan, and you work out the details of the hospital. They are not involved in working out the budget costs and the detail of the hospital, they leave that to us, but they are involved in the approval in principle of the big projects. Their main interest there is in satisfying themselves that there has been proper investment appraisal.

His opposite number at the Treasury, George Monger, the Under Secretary in charge of health spending, offers the same figure, but a subtly different nuance. It's not so much a question of when the Treasury gets involved, as when ministers do.

Monger:

Generally speaking, health and social security matters involve so much money and such sensitive political consider-ations that they have to be referred to ministers. I don't say that's true of every single thing, but I think it's true of the generality of things, but I can give an example of something which might not be referred to ministers, if you want one. The DHSS have to get our agreement to starting any major capital project in the NHS of a total cost of £10 million or above, a major hospital, for example. Normally speaking, something like that might not be referred to ministers; a lot would depend on where the hospital was, if there were any important local considerations, that sort of thing.

Over at Defence, the considerations – and the figure – seem to be rather different.

Bryars:

It varies from field to field. I would say that in the manpower field Treasury supervision has to be tighter than elsewhere. There are obvious reasons for that: no one Whitehall department can act on its own – whatever one Whitehall department does in the question of pay and conditions of service and manpower affects other Whitehall departments. It also has a knock-on effect elsewhere in the public sector – for the police, for example. So in that area the Treasury has to keep a pretty close interest in what is going on. Elsewhere the degree of supervision is not so tight: for defence equipment we have the discretion to go ahead with projects which are under £25 million, which leaves quite a lot that does go to the Treasury. But the Treasury is quite open to discussion about what the right level of delegation should be. They have no interest themselves in getting more work than they can absorb – there's no point in that – they couldn't deal with it properly, and we wouldn't get the best value out of it. So if we think that the shoe is pinching particularly hard in a particular area, and we can explain this to the Treasury, they are quite amenable to argument about whether the level of delegation should be raised.

Even at the Treasury, surprisingly, the system by which it retains the final say, ultimately through its ministers, is not reckoned perfectly satisfactory. Peter Middleton, Permanent Secretary designate, hardly doubts that Treasury control is desirable. But he concedes that it is attacked, justly, for interfering too much.

Middleton:

I think that's a fair criticism, and it must always look that way to departments. I think there'll be occasions when we actually do do that, but it's all part of this balance that we're talking about: of trying to get enough information to do the job in the Treasury, to make the departments feel you're always there, so that there is a sort of hand behind them when they're taking their spending decisions, but not interfering to the point where they feel they haven't got the responsibility for the actual expenditure, which they have. So I've no doubt it looks that way to departments at times, but equally at times it can look here as though we don't interfere enough.

Or, as Anthony Rawlinson delphically puts it, when asked whether the Treasury is concerned with the quality of public spending.

Rawlinson:

Concerned, yes. Directly responsible, no. That is, on the whole, the responsibility of departments, though I don't wish to imply that the Treasury washes its hands of it. It does not.

An impression confirmed by at least one former big-spending minister, Peter Shore. Did he find the Treasury constantly trying to interfere in detail?

Shore:

No, not in my experience. The big battle was always the grand strategy involving the total of public expenditure. As far as the Treasury was concerned, with their sweating brows at the end of that stage, once departments in a state of near exhaustion had agreed what they would spend, they were only too pleased to leave to individual departments the distribution of the sums of money within their own separate areas of responsibility.

An image of titanic combat which also emerges from one Treasury man who brought the process down to its basics: Nicholas Monck, Under Secretary in the Home Finance Group.

Monck:

Because the Treasury has less power over public expenditure than it does in some other countries, you always end up having to say 'no' and having to cut wherever you can. As a Frenchman put it to me once, 'As a finance man you sometimes have to be stupid'. You don't actually have the power to say we're going to get to a desirable total by a combination of expanding some things which clearly have a good economic case and knocking out this other rubbish; you have in practice to take a cut wherever you can get it.

Even to achieve that much, however, the Treasury needs a way of monitoring its sums, and in particular the public sector borrowing requirement – the gap between all public spending and all public revenue. The methods of maintaining knowledge and control over these figures have preoccupied generations of mandarins. For quite a long time spending wasn't really planned at all, in the modern sense.

Planning began in earnest in the early 1960s with the introduction of public expenditure surveys called PESC,[1] published

---

1 The introduction of Public Expenditure Surveys was first recommended in *The Plowden Report* (Cmnd. 1432), HMSO, 1961.

annually, but looking some years ahead, to try and match spending and resources. But inflation made this system fall apart in the end; at one point it was even discovered that £6000 million appeared to have been lost in the accounts. Because all these plans were expressed in constant prices – as though inflation had never entered the picture – they began to run wildly out of line with the real money available. The money even came to be called 'funny money', and it's as a result of this that we have the famous system of cash limits, first introduced by the Labour government in 1976.[1] Two years ago they were further developed and Geoffrey Howe announced that all spending plans would henceforth be expressed in actual cash figures, with an inflation prediction built in.[2]

That last, neat little paragraph encapsulates in half a minute literally thousands of man-hours of high-level thinking and debate about how to tame the beast in the public purse. It is almost shameful to have done such little justice to the profundity of effort! But that is the pith of the matter, and it has given the Treasury more control – £6000 million won't be lost again in a hurry. Almost, from some people's point of view, it has too much control. Hand in hand with cash limits goes a stubborn persistence in separating each year from every other. Budget for one year, spend in one year. That's what the departments are told. Hence the startling order not long ago to local authorities to spend a quick billion because the Environment Department was undershooting its budget.[3] Hence, also, big problems for departments with long-term programmes – like, as Sir Frank Cooper briskly recalls, Defence.

Cooper:

As far as most defence is concerned, because of the asinine annuality system that we run the country on, if we suddenly lost a hundred million pounds, in terms of our programme which is planned in periods of ten years – and you carry that through – that is one billion pounds, which is a whole major weapon system. Now that is why we argue very hard, and we do argue hard, because we work on a ten-year

---

1 Public Expenditure White Paper (Cmnd. 6393), HMSO, 1976.
2 Budget Speech of 10 March 1981, *Official Report*, HC, Vol. 1000, no. 64, col. 768.
3 The likely underspend was first announced by the Secretary of State, Michael Heseltine, in a written answer on 27 October 1983, *Official Report*, HC, Vol. 29, no. 174, col. 455.

system, and if we lose so many million pounds to the Treasury we've got then to carry it through our long-term costings, and out of the window has got to go something which we hold dear.

At the Treasury, Leon Brittan denies that annuality is a doctrine.

Brittan:

It's a matter of practicality in that we do have annual budgets, both for spending and for revenue, and you've got to know what is going to happen in a particular year. Now, we have been looking at schemes which would blur that and enable a greater degree of flexibility, but there is always a cost in terms of extra expenditure incurred that would otherwise not occur – which is, after all, why everyone wants it. And also a cost in terms of loss of discipline, but I certainly wouldn't want you to think that there's any sort of Treasury dogma about it.

And even Frank Cooper concedes that there would be perils in going over to a new system.

Cooper:

Well, let me be fair to the Treasury, which I always find difficult but I do actually try. I have got some sympathy with them on this because intellectually they have no arguments left, they're stripped to their underpants, without any doubt in my view. But for the first time for a very long period they have actually got public expenditure under control; they do not want to lose control and I would support them one hundred per cent in that. For many, many years they've been holding back the dam but now they've actually propped it up, I think, and they don't want to let the water through again. So their problem is how to move over from one system to another system; it's basically a problem of timing and/or procedure, rather than one of policy, quite frankly.[1]

---

1 The problem of timing and procedure was solved on 7 July 1983 when Sir Geoffrey Howe's successor as Chancellor, Nigel Lawson, announced to the House of Commons in the course of a statement about public expenditure cuts: 'A scheme of end-year cash limits flexibility will be introduced. This will permit some carry-forward of underspend on central government capital programmes. Such a change has, of course, long been advocated by departments such as the Ministry of Defence, with substantial capital programmes involving expenditure stretching over a number of years. The change, I believe, is fully justified on managerial grounds, but introducing it as from this financial year should, in practice, by reducing the end-year surge, reduce expenditure in the current year by some £100m.' *Official Report*, HC, Vol. 45, no. 16. col. 418, 7 July 1983.

At the back of this, however, are the politicians. Control may be the Treasury's key job but choices are the Cabinet's. It is in the choice of priorities for public spending that governments may most differ from each other. This is collective decision-making as the textbooks say it should be – although, as Leon Brittan says, the choice at Cabinet level can only be very broad.

Brittan:

What happens is that the government determines its broad priorities as to what expenditure should be, and those are obviously reviewed from time to time. Then I, as Chief Secretary, put to the Cabinet my views as to what the totality of spending should be, and also give a broad picture of how it is broken down. Those figures are affirmed, disagreed with, amended or whatever, and then I have to go back and engage in the annual review, that is the more difficult task of squaring the circle and actually making the individual programmes fit. I then have to report back to Cabinet. If I'm unable to reach an agreement which is satisfactory to me and to the spending minister, that particular disagreement can be referred to Cabinet or some committee of the Cabinet; and if I'm unable to stick within the total that the Cabinet had agreed, it could occur that I would ask Cabinet to revise that total.

In 1980 and 1981 there were some pretty stormy scenes as the Thatcher Cabinet divided over how much to keep spending down. But this year, it seemed, the process had been completed without need to refer to a single Cabinet committee.

Brittan:

That is correct, yes.[1]

How very different from the last Labour government – a government, remember, with no overall desire to cut spending, and with warring ministers trying all the time to fight the Treasury's arithmetic. As Tony Benn describes it, Cabinet discussion was not very like the textbook.

---

1 The emergency measures on public expenditure announced by Nigel Lawson on 7 July 1983 appear to have been negotiated in a less organised manner. The statement cut the Defence Budget by £230 million less than the figures published in the Defence White Paper twenty-four hours earlier. Asked about the sudden change, the Defence Secretary, Michael Heseltine, said: 'I knew there would be a discussion today, but I had no means of knowing what the outcome would be.' (*The Times*, 8 July 1983). Peter Shore commented in the House of Commons (*Official Report*, HC, Vol. 45, no. 16, col. 419): 'Is this not a classic example of a Treasury panic and a Cabinet bounce?'

Benn:

What would happen is the Chancellor would come with bids for cuts far greater than he knew he'd get, and the Prime Minister no doubt would privately decide how far he'd go along with the Chancellor, and the Chancellor knew he wouldn't get everything he wanted, and ministers would come intending to defend everything that affected their department, and there was a slight element of fiasco about it.

This resolved itself into bilateral meetings between the Treasury and individual departments – which is where the process began to smack of a Whitehall plot.

Benn:

The Treasury would plan in its bilateral meeting to get much more from a minister than they knew they could get and this is where the element of collusion comes in with the civil servants in the minister's own department. Before you went, there would be discussions between, say, my civil servants at the Department of Energy or Industry and the Treasury. There would be a lot of horse-trading, but it's at this point that your own officials would be able to offer up as part of the deal the projects that might be dear to the minister, but that they'd never really liked, and then they would give you a brief as to what the Chancellor would ask. It took me a long time to appreciate what was going on – to begin with you'd think it was a real battle, but actually the thing had been pre-fixed by officials to some extent.

From elsewhere in that government, things did not look quite the same. Peter Shore was Secretary of State for the Environment and found his civil servants actually fulfilling neither the Benn image of devious conspirators, nor, it should be said, the image of Sir Kenneth Stowe – that of the government as one big, united, loyal family.

Shore:

My civil servants acted wholly as though they were servants of the Secretary of State for the Environment, rather than part of the collectivity of the civil service, and that went just as much for civil servants who had once served in the Treasury as it did for those who had served only in spending departments. I found throughout my period in office that my civil servants, at any rate, were very pleased indeed when I succeeded in warding off the Treasury. And in providing a whole system of fortification against Treasury assault they were anxious to equip me, to fight just as well in the third trench back as I had been fighting in the front line.

A textbook description, which Joan Kelley fully endorses.

Kelley:

The present practice on public expenditure control, on the whole, allows considerable freedom for a minister to fix his own priorities. I say 'considerable freedom' because it isn't absolute. You couldn't, for example, have Sir Keith Joseph deciding that he would abolish compulsory schooling in favour of spending all the money on something else. That would be a matter for a political decision by the Cabinet but, on the whole, we take the view that departments should be able to decide their own priorities and that they can make a better assessment of their own priorities than could ever be forced upon them by the Treasury from the outside.

But, at bottom, is there not necessarily a bias against public spending at the Treasury? Is this not its inescapable role, in the dialogue which defines a government's direction: that same dialogue which occurs in one way or another, in every kind of government under the sun? Anthony Rawlinson, who came closer to the classic model of Treasury mandarin than anyone else we came across, delicately admitted the Treasury's prejudice.

Rawlinson:

It's true in most circumstances, and it has certainly been true during the period when I've been in charge of the public expenditure side, that there is always pressure from spending departments in aggregate to spend more than the government as a whole would wish to spend on public expenditure. So, certainly, the Treasury has a traditional and proper concern to hold a sceptical attitude towards public expenditure in general, although we are perfectly capable of taking a constructive view about particular projects. I think we are also conscious, on the public expenditure side, of our duty to the government and to the taxpayers to promote value for money.

Frank Cooper, characteristically, put it with greater bluntness.

Cooper:

You've got to go back to the fact that they are run by their ministers to a degree which, quite frankly, I do not believe any other department in Whitehall is. The whole centrepiece of any government is the question of what it is going to do about spending. Is it going to spend more? Is it going to spend less? They take their tune almost totally from that, and they must do. They then go round and invent good reasons why what emerges is a good policy or a bad policy. But the tune comes out by the minister of the day – that's the Chancellor of the Exchequer and the Prime Minister basically – pressing the button on public expenditure, backed up by the feeling of whichever party's in government.

It is on to ministers that Peter Middleton too, very naturally, wants to deflect the onus. But he came close to gentle outrage at the suggestion that, in the politics of Whitehall, the Chancellor of the Exchequer must, in all circumstances, neither initiate nor favour higher public spending.

Middleton:

Oh, no, I don't think that's at all true. It may be a little true of the Chief Secretary in the Treasury, who is the minister who is always responsible for controlling expenditure, so one would expect him to be the man who said 'no' nine times out of ten. I think that would apply whatever sort of public expenditure programme the government had. Some governments want expenditure lower than others, but none want it completely out of control. So there has to be somebody there who is keeping it as high as you want or as low as you want, and in recent times that unfortunate job has devolved on the Chief Secretary. It would be a difficult job to be a popular minister and be Chief Secretary. But the Treasury as a whole and the Chancellor don't see things that way. Keeping public expenditure down in a general sense is always part of the work, but there will be times when you want particular programmes, and particular parts of public expenditure, to grow at the expense of others. That's an essential part of economic management and just as essential as having particular taxes growing or contracting. It's all part of the general process of keeping both the macro-economy and the micro-economy in a healthy state.

To this task, many high-powered Treasury men and women devote themselves. The place has, as we've already noted, got its own distinct and rather proud ethos: and attitudes to public spending are one major element in that. Much of what's been said so far makes this part of the job sound pretty unsatisfactory, all too much like that of an impotent middleman. But George Monger doesn't agree.

Monger:

The professional satisfaction is really to get to understand these enormous programmes which involve a lot of money and a lot of political consideration, really to get to the bottom of them in so far as it's possible for us to do so, and then to present the results of our thinking and researches and discussions with DHSS and Treasury ministers. What's more, although the big decisions are inevitably made by Treasury ministers, we advise them, we present and order the material for them, and we generally help them to come to their decisions. That involves quite a major effort when you've got programmes as big and as complicated as the Social Security and Health programmes, and that is in itself satisfying.

But is the Treasury ethos a lifetime affliction? While we were making the programmes, a sizeable reshuffle was announced in Whitehall, sending several top Treasury people out to run some of the spending departments.[1] A major extension of Treasury rigour, surely? Sir Douglas Wass had few illusions.

Wass:

No, I don't think it means any extension of the Treasury's power at all. This is not the first time that senior Treasury people have been exported to head other departments, spending departments. In my personal experience ex-Treasury people are the worst possible spenders, they're the biggest enemies the Treasury has – they know exactly how the Treasury functions and they're able to beat us at our own game, putting it very crudely. I can give many examples of that – I won't, as this is a public occasion – but I wouldn't expect any of the ex-Treasury people who go out to spend money, to do other than the best for their ministers and their departments.

So there is no Treasury mind, trained in perpetuity to take a

---

1 They were: Sir Kenneth Couzens who became Permanent Secretary at the Department of Energy on 1 January 1983; Sir Anthony Rawlinson who became Permanent Secretary at the Department of Trade on 28 April 1983; and David Hancock who became Permanent Secretary at the Department of Education and Science on 3 May 1983. Sir William Ryrie had already left the Treasury to become Permanent Secretary of the Overseas Development Administration at the Foreign and Commonwealth Office on 16 April 1982.

Treasury attitude. There is a network of competing interests. And the Treasury is not above the battle, but necessarily a participant. The real choices are, or should be, made elsewhere. But Chancellors of the Exchequer, like Denis Healey, do not easily succeed in persuading the Cabinet to make, in rational and godlike fashion, the choices we all might understand as the real ones. Should we, for example, have another motorway – or would five new hospitals be better?

Healey:

I think the real problem is that, first of all, Chancellors rarely interfere as between spending on one thing or another inside departments. The most difficult problems which governments face are deciding as between one department and another, and I tried very hard when I was Chancellor to invent systems of organisation which would enable the Cabinet to decide priorities as between for example, health, education and housing. But somehow or other that never really worked out quite right. I think the most difficult thing is to get a Cabinet to take a decision on priorities between departments, partly because you have to stop the machine in order to have time to think – and stopping the machine is very difficult.

For all the present harmony of the Thatcher government, choice-making is not really any cooler or more rational now. The language of priorities, however grand it sounds, is never terribly clear. Most public spending is preordained years or even decades ago. It's on the margin, as Sir Frank Cooper said, that the direction can change. And in that process the Treasury, despite protestations to the contrary, will always have a bias against an increase. In the end, that's its role. Somebody has to do it. But somebody – many people around Whitehall – make sure from time to time that it does not always get its way.

The Budget Makers

First Broadcast: 13 March 1983

The images of place associated with the Budget are, we like to think, familiar. The first is a snapshot on the steps of Number 11 Downing Street. The Chancellor of the Exchequer emerges from his official residence, ritually grinning and holding up the same old battered red box which, year after year, is supposed to carry the Budget secrets. The second comes an hour or two later. We are in the House of Commons. The place is packed to the doors; not an inch of the tasteful green leather benches is visible. Humming expectantly, the House waits until the Chancellor finally rises and then, after an hour or more of ponderous economic analysis, swiftly deals out the tax changes to catch the late evening paper headlines.

It's all very traditional, even reassuring. But as a piece of dramatic truth it is decidedly misleading. Let's examine another image, from where the Budget really begins.

The place is a computer room: a new, brightly lit, modern room in an old building, where the green on the walls is a rather tasteless shade of lime. Here the hum is inhuman, and it never ceases. There are a few people about – the bright-eyed boffin types you seem to find at computer installations everywhere. This is the Treasury computer room, and we are in the presence of the nearest thing you can find to the physical embodiment of the Treasury model – that famous, or infamous, structure of economic equations, the massive study of which does so much to dictate what, in fact, the Chancellor appears to be so coolly reeling off in the House. The Chancellor himself, Sir Geoffrey Howe, seems to feel he's in a theatre.

Howe:

One feels rather like an actor-manager on the first night of a play he's written himself, subject to the overriding condition that nine-tenths of the plot is settled by the world in advance anyway.

Do things ever go wrong? The Permanent Secretary, Sir Douglas Wass.

Wass:

Oh yes, things can go wrong wherever human activity is concerned. But it's a well-rehearsed exercise in the sense that we've had many Budgets before, and many people doing any one Budget have done a previous Budget and therefore are aware of all the loose ends. There is also a great manual of guidance on the Budget which each new generation of Budget makers can refer to. It goes into considerable detail about points that have got to be covered: how many copies of this paper are produced, what time this is to be released, when the Press are to be involved, when the Chancellor is to see the Lobby, and so on and so forth. Now all this helps to avoid the making of a mistake but, nevertheless, there's something new in every Budget which can expose one to the possibility of error.

But the Chancellor reckons this is only the very smallest possibility. Could things ever go wrong?

Howe:

They can, I suppose. I go into the House of Commons and find I've not got the speech in the magic box or something, and that would cause a certain *frisson*. Or the actual speech itself might go wrong, or small things can go wrong, but in general it doesn't seem to have happened.[1]

Our discussion is not about this year's Budget. It's about how the Treasury goes about making the Budget – the process and its bearing on the total effect of budgets: the Budget judgement, as it's called. That's what the Budget really is: a major statement of economic policy and, as such, prone to both error and continuing revision. At one extreme, indeed, if you're really blasé, Budget Day itself might seem overrated. Peter Kemp,[2] a rare bird in the Treasury, being a qualified accountant and having no university degree, is the Under Secretary in charge of the central unit, where the Budget operation is co-ordinated.

---

1 In this Budget on 15 March 1983 something did go wrong. A member of the Central Unit Staff spent hours researching in the Treasury archives to trace the date of the longest Budget speech for Sir Geoffrey's opening sentence. *Hansard* reported what happened:

The Chancellor of the Exchequer (Sir Geoffrey Howe): The longest Budget speech that I have been able to trace was given by Mr Gladstone on 18 April 1953 – (*Interruption*)

Mr Deputy Speaker: Order. Perhaps the Chancellor would like to start again.

Sir Geoffrey Howe: I am content, Mr Deputy Speaker, to recognise that, although Liberals have long lives, they do not live that long. The date to which I refer, of course, was 1853. (*Official Report*, HC, Vol. 39, no. 79, col. 134, 15 March 1983.)

2 Peter Kemp was promoted to Deputy Secretary in charge of the pay sector in May 1983.

Kemp:

In one sense I think you should say that Budgets never really stop and never really start. There is a continuing, ongoing process of ministerial economic policy-making. This government has published its medium-term financial strategy,[1] and that's an ongoing strategy. The numbers in it may be revised from time to time, but the strategy of getting down inflation and restoring output in that way is an ongoing business, and doesn't really come to a head necessarily at any particular time.

Even so, as one of Kemp's subordinates, David Norgrove, adds,

Norgrove:

It does help to have this one day of the year, a kind of terminus, on which you have to make a major presentation of the government's economic policies, which then becomes a 'locus classicus' for the rest of the year.

An impression confirmed by the Chancellor himself.

Howe:

The Treasury regards the Budget as one of the major policy-forming exercises of the year. There's a tremendous commitment of effort; the preparation goes on over many months, starting probably before the Budget before last, as it were. There is therefore great tension, and an enthusiasm and interest in it, which I think the Chancellor shares. It is a very important piece of economic policy-making.

The process does actually begin a long time before the Budget – shortly after the last one, in fact – with the preliminary discussions about next year's public spending. After that's been fixed, along the lines already described, debate turns to the Budget: tax-raising, monetary policy, government borrowing and all the other components, with all their constantly varying effects, of economic management. Long before the Chancellor himself gets involved, composing those emphatic declarations and firm prophecies we hear on Budget Day, the first people to come into their own are the economists, who spend their time mapping and observing this teeming entity called the British economy on the Treasury model – an abstract thing, now crisply rendered more real by the economist in charge of macro-economic policy analysis, Rachel Lomax.

---

1 The medium-term financial strategy was published in the *Financial Statement and Budget Report 1981/82*, HC Paper 237.

Lomax:

At the physical level it's just a computer programme with a lot of equations – quite a lot of equations, about seven hundred in the case of the Treasury model. And the equations represent an attempt to describe the workings of the economy in terms of economically meaningful numerical relationships.

Meaningful maybe, but are they scientific?

Lomax:

I think to pretend that you can achieve anything like the precision that you can in the physical sciences is obviously quite wrong. There's a lot of art in it as well, and I think the people who build models and use them are more conscious of the limitations of the models than the rest of the world. We have quite modest claims for what models can do. We would regard them, I guess, as a framework for thinking about rather complicated problems rather than as a sort of oracle – the sort you see in science fiction films, where you go and ask, 'What will happen if . . .?' and the model tells you the answer. We would never treat it that literally, it's just a tool.

It is on this vastly complex computerised network that forecasts can, nevertheless, be tested for what effects certain Budget measures might have on other economic facts. Computers, you see, are like science fiction – at least to this extent. They can keep fifty balls in the air at once. Rachel Lomax again.

Lomax:

If I wanted to know, for example, what the effect of changing tax allowances was – the Chancellor was thinking about doing that in the Budget and he asked me what would be the effect[1] – I would have to start from the forecast, that would give me a base. I'd have to formulate a rather precise question – it's very important to ask the right questions if you're going to get a sensible answer – so I would have to ask the computer what would be the effect of changing these tax allowances on the assumption, for example, that the exchange rate is free to float, on the assumption that the

---

1 In the event the Chancellor did announce changes in tax allowances in the 1983 Budget, increasing the tax threshold for a single person to £1785 and for a married person to £2795. He also made small increases in personal and age allowances.

government is pursuing a fixed interest rate or a fixed money supply policy, on a range of assumptions about how the government behaves when the rest of the economy changes. We then do another computer run and it prints out a new version of the forecast, but most usefully it works out conveniently for us what the difference from the original forecast was. It will show the effect on output, on employment, on the PSBR, or on the exchange rate – whatever it is that I'm particularly interested in – and then typically I would sit and puzzle and decide whether I liked the answer and believed it.

That last point is very important. Treasury economists have visual display terminals on their desks and can get an instant read-out on the model. New laser printing can produce a complete print-out of, for example, a five-year projection running to 120 pages, in one minute. But after that flash of super technology, picture Rachel Lomax sitting back and deciding whether she liked what the forecast said – a picture further coloured in by the Permanent Secretary-elect, Peter Middleton.

Middleton:

Looked at from the outside, I think the usual view is that the forecast is produced by a lot of robots stuck in the basement, and takes the form of fancy-dress mathematical equations of one sort or another, but of course that's not the case. A lot of hard work, a lot of research and a lot of estimation goes into producing the basic equations in the model, but it's done against a shifting world where relationships break down at any time, and the number of relationships which are actually fully estimated is very, very small indeed. The process which the forecasters go through is to apply judgement to that; they don't quite believe what their equations are saying, we wouldn't want to employ them if they did.

Even under the present government, when detailed forecasting and fine-tuning of the economy is mistrusted, the model and its message are a vital tool.

Middleton:

If you're not in a fine-tuning regime, you're still interested in the effect of particular policy measures and in the relationship between them. The model, I think, is probably at its most valuable when it's not being used to forecast, but producing the answers to those sorts of things. For example, if you take the present set of monetary policies, it's of crucial importance to know how particular changes in the borrowing requirement affect interest rates and the exchange rate and the money supply itself, as well as prices and output in the economy at large. Now you can't sit down with the back of an envelope and try to analyse that sort of thing – you need a system which will trace those flows through the financial system, through the whole apparatus, to give you an idea of what you're doing. That's a very, very important part of the process.

It seems, however, that the Thatcher government did momentarily contemplate the radical step of abandoning a lot of this mumbo-jumbo. Andrew Britton, who's just left a senior position in the Treasury to become director of the National Institute for Economic and Social Research, blows the gaffe.

Britton:

Well, it was seriously discussed that we might stop forecasting, that the government's approach no longer needed forecasts because they were no longer fine-tuning. Part of the difficulty about dropping it would be that it is now a semi-public activity.[1] But in any case it was recognised, and is recognised, that the forecasts are essential to the process of decision-making within the government, whatever the framework of the strategy. For example, the government has recently been putting great emphasis on the public sector borrowing requirement as a measure of the room to manoeuvre in fiscal policy, so one needs to forecast what the public sector borrowing requirement will be on existing policies before one can say how much scope for manoeuvre there is. Forecasting the public sector borrowing requirement is no easier than forecasting what's going to happen to the level of activity over the next year. Indeed, it's a good deal more difficult, and forecasting the level of activity is a necessary step on the way to trying to forecast the public sector borrowing requirement. So it is technically necessary to go on forecasting even if you don't think it's politically necessary directly to know what the level of activity is, or appropriate for the government to try and control it.

---

1 The Treasury forecasts are published twice a year, in the *Financial Statement and Budget Report* which accompanies the Budget statement, and in the *Autumn Statement*. The Treasury model is also publicly accessible for use by outside bodies through commercial computer bureaux.

For behind the irrefutable statistics from the past, which do form the major basis for estimating the future, is the unpredictability of coming events – oil prices, farm deals in Brussels, exchange rate and the rest – which all require of forecasters and ministers, as Douglas Wass says, human judgement.

Wass:

Some of the judgements are necessarily little more than guesses, and guesses in which there's no element of professional expertise. A professional economist who's trained in econometrics is no better at guessing what the Brussels Commissioners are going to recommend on the next CAP price increase than I am or you are. Now, when we discuss the forecast among ourselves as officials and with ministers, we frequently do look at some of these more tenuous assumptions and ministers will, like any customer, look at the validity of some of those assumptions. They'll also look at some assumptions where there is perhaps some professional input, but where there's also a great deal of judgement being made. In all those areas, at every level of discussion, whether one's professionally qualified or not, there is room for argument as to whether the right assumption has been made. And in those areas ministers may express scepticism or doubt about particular assumptions, may say, 'Well, wouldn't it be . . . isn't it more likely to be, this?' And we'd talk about the possibility that it would be this rather than that, and may change the forecast somewhat. So there is scope, I think, for the lay consumer of a forecast to challenge the product even though it is a professionally-produced product.

For this process, half science and half seat-of-the-pants, it's ultimately ministers who carry the can. The forecast can add up to high politics. It mustn't look absurd and, according to Andrew Britton, it mustn't, preferably, look too depressing to the masses outside.

Britton:

What the discussion actually, in practice, consists of very largely is the question 'what is the range of outside views?' And if ministers feel that the Treasury forecasters themselves are putting forward a view which is perhaps rather pessimistic relative to the average public forecast, they may well say that they would prefer to see something more optimistic. That's the sort of thing that goes on.

There had been times when the business had become thoroughly suspect.

Britton:

There was a time in which ministers attempted to have it both ways – they tried to change the numbers and to disown them. But that is not the current practice. The current practice is that ministers do play some role in deciding what the numbers should be and they then take responsibility for them.

The irreverent thought did occur to us that since the forecasts are so often wrong, were in any case bound to be uncertain, and were now controlled by ministers who had set their face against old-fashioned fine-tuning of the economy every time it slid out of line with the forecast – perhaps too much time was spent on them. Peter Middleton soon put us right.

Middleton:

You never know exactly where you are now when you're doing a forecast, and, of course, you never quite know how the rest of the world is doing. It's difficult enough to forecast your own economy without forecasting the rest of the world. There are times, as this time last year, where just about everybody in the world got their forecasts wrong; they all got inflation too high and output too high. But I don't think that's a reason for saying, 'Oh well, we can do just as well on the back of an envelope'. You can't. I think it makes a good deal of sense just to regard the forecast as contributing to your understanding of the economy. Anybody who runs his economic policy on the assumption that the forecast numbers are going to be right, when the only thing you know for sure is that they're not going to be, wants his head examined. But we don't do that.

Besides, whatever the doubts, there are, as Peter Kemp reminds us, decisions to be made.

Kemp:

The forecasters, if they were living in an ivory tower, as so many of the commentators are, would like to say, 'Well, we think that the public expenditure borrowing requirement ought to be this or possibly that, and there may be some four or five billion pounds difference between the two', and they'd give a bracket. Unfortunately, real life isn't like that. One actually has to work to a spot figure, one actually has to decide what one's going to do if one is going to reduce a given tax; whatever it is, it has a cost and that has to be measured.

So the big picture is as clear as it can be. A forecast is fixed; some of the large judgements about how much expansion or contraction to provide for, how much borrowing, how much inflation, are beginning to disclose themselves. Uncertainty is resolved by the need to choose and to act.

On these choices, the Treasury is never short of advice. The Budget is the great annual moment towards which every kind of interest group, from licensed victuallers to pensioners, through building societies, child poverty people, stockbrokers and even actors and theatre managers, directs its lobby for change favourable to itself: which, naturally, it also manages to reconcile with the larger national interest. What weight these interest groups have varies from government to government. In present times, for example, the CBI, led by Sir Terence Beckett, seems to be in and out of the Treasury every week.

Beckett:

The meetings we have with them are really quite frequent during the year. It's a mistake to think we have one meeting just before the Budget, for example, to talk about the representations we've got on that subject. There are meetings taking place all through the year with Sir Geoffrey Howe, with his principal ministers in the Treasury and with Treasury officials. The meetings involve a variety of representatives from the CBI, for example, the President, its members, the Chairman of the Economic Policy Committee, and sometimes our officials here in conjunction with their officials.

Sir Terence told us he personally saw the Chancellor once or twice a month, interspersed with numerous telephone calls. At the TUC these days, says its Assistant General Secretary, David Lea, it's a rather different story.

Lea:

Under this government I think we can say that we can count on the fingers of one hand the amount of contact we've had. It's quite extraordinary actually, the contrast not only, if I may say so, with the Labour government – there is a point to be made there as well, I'm sure – but with previous Conservative governments. The freeze on relations with the TUC has been very marked.

Despite this, the present government has made a concession to the outside world by publishing some proposals for it to comment on.[1] These are vague and not hugely revealing but they begin to constitute a kind of 'green budget', such as was recommended by the Treasury and Civil Service Committee at the House of Commons,[2] of which Labour MP Michael Meacher is a prominent member.

Meacher:

I think one area where we clearly have had an effect is in the demand – in which, of course, we were only reflecting the views of the Armstrong Committee[3] – that there should be what is called a 'green budget'. In other words, that the budgetary options should be discussed openly at the end of the year well before the Budget in March/April, so that not just this tiny, élite clique of officials and ministers in the Treasury should make these major decisions which affect the lives of us all, but that it should be thrown open so far as possible. I mean, obviously not tax changes, but broad decisions affecting the running of the whole economy – we should see what the options are. Now we did put that forward, and for the first time this year we have had something approximating to a green budget. I would say that's not perfect, that's not all we wanted, but given the resistance of Treasury officials in evidence to that, I think we've got most and rather more than we expected. I'd say we've got three-quarters of what we expected. I think it's something on which we can build; we shall chip away and try to get more.

The question is, however, do ministers pay any real attention to the numerous Budget submissions made by MPs and others before Budget decisions are finally made? We rather gathered that little of what anyone says comes exactly as a surprise to the mandarins. Officials like Peter Middleton sound as though they've heard most of it before.

---

1 In an *Autumn Statement* (HC Paper 10, 8 November 1982), which set out likely public expenditure and revenue figures for the coming year and the array of choices open to the Chancellor.
2 The recommendation was, in fact, made by two Committees of the House: the Treasury and Civil Service Committee, Second Special Report of 1981/82 Session, HC Paper 521; and the Procedure (Finance) Select Committee 1982/83, First Report, HC Paper 24.
3 *Budgetary Reform in the UK*. Report of the Committee chaired by Lord Armstrong of Sanderstead. Published by the OUP for the Institute of Fiscal Studies, 1980.

Middleton:

Some of it, I suppose, goes on all the time. I mean, it is very important in an organisation like the Treasury to get out and meet people, but you can't get out and meet everybody, the world is too large, so you do tend to spend a fair bit of your time talking to organisations which represent groups of people – and that seems to me to be a very important part of not leading a totally ivory-tower existence. Now at Budget time, of course, the scale of that sort of thing increases quite considerably. The main thing that happens is that, starting in about September the previous year, which is when the budgetary process really begins, one gets an absolute deluge of representations, and these, by and large, are of two sorts. One consists of advice on the way people think the government ought to run the economy, and advice of that sort is most noticeable from bodies like the TUC, the CBI, the Institute of Directors and various academic institutes – a lot of advice of that sort, which is all very valuable, is taken into account, and changes as the year goes on.

Then you get another lot which is advice about what people would like to do with particular taxes, and you very rarely get advice in the direction of increasing taxes. It's almost all tax reductions. Some of it is very predictable. You know that the Scotch Whisky manufacturers aren't going to suggest you put up the tax on Scotch, and that tobacco manufacturers aren't going to suggest you put up the tax on tobacco, and the child poverty action group aren't going to suggest you increase the poverty trap. Nonetheless, all these things are gone through and sifted for two things: one, to see if the arguments have changed, or whether the weight of the arguments has changed – and sometimes they will have, sometimes they won't – because, in particular, different industries go through different phases of profitability and otherwise; and secondly, to see what they say.

Now all these representations are painstakingly summarised. They are put to ministers, and the Budget proposals are usually divided into two lists: one which is described as 'minor starts', not because they're not important but because they don't cost a vast amount of money, and the other of which is called 'major things for the Budget', which affect the whole macro-economy. They're sifted through by ministers and officials to decide which one fits into the strategy,

75

which ones might be starters, and which ones might carry on. Now, of course ministers might ask you to go and talk to particular groups to find out exactly what they're saying – sometimes it's not totally clear – or they might have ideas of their own that they want you to try out on them. So officials do have a function but it's a sort of joint ministerial function. In the course of this, I suppose, there are people who are busily trying to bend your ear, but I don't mind that particularly – that goes with the job. If you want information, you've got to allow people to give you opinions, too.

Only the very specialist groups, it would seem from Douglas Wass, really have a chance of changing the Treasury's all-seeing mind.

Wass:

You have to remember that we are in continuous contact with the large pressure groups, so we know how their thinking is evolving over time, and their Budget representations never come to us as a complete surprise. We've had talks with them over the years, their thinking is evolutionary, there's not a step-jump in it as a rule, so it is comparatively rare, for instance, for the Tobacco Advisory Council to put in a Budget representation which takes us by surprise. Nevertheless, there are occasions when a body, a pressure group, has taken its thinking a little farther without disclosing it to us, and does produce what you call a new idea. That's certainly possible. I think we would claim that we do take notice of all these people, particularly where representation is being made to us by a rather specialist body. For example, a body dealing with contract hire equipment, which may have views about the functioning of some credit mechanism or the functioning of some allowance system in the fiscal code. In that case, what they have to say about the impact of the monetary system or the fiscal system on their ability to sell competitively in the Third World markets would be of very considerable interest to us, and of course we'd listen to them.

Peter Middleton made a similar point.

Middleton:

You very rarely get new ideas about macro-economic management when a government has been in power for a while, but what you do get is plenty of new ideas about taxation. I should say the problem really is that there are far too many new ideas. The difficulty is deciding which ones to take seriously. I think that's bound to be true if you've got a tax system which is as complicated as ours, and where there is always scope for simplification. The Treasury itself, if I can speak for it for a moment, will always try to give as much time as it can to anything which simplifies both sides of the Budget – the benefit side and the tax side. One can devise a nice idealised system which would vastly simplify the Budget process: by taking out a lot of tax anomalies on one side and a lot of tax allowances on the other side, combining that with the Social Security system and producing a much more simple system. We like to think we're moving in that direction, but of course it's not the sort of thing you can do overnight. That's a long-term objective, but one within which there's room for plenty of fertile ideas.

Rich and varied as the range of access to the Treasury at Budget time is, not everyone there is wholly happy that the process is fair and even-handed. Under Secretary Peter Kemp thinks it could even cause a serious distortion.

Kemp:

I mean, one example is the case of industry versus persons. One of the greatest arguments that comes up with every single Budget is, what are the relative priorities – in so far as there are reliefs to be given – as between things that might help industry and things that might help persons? It's curious that although we have, for instance, a big industrial lobby, people like the Confederation of British Industry, there isn't really much of a lobby for individuals. I've often thought that if there was a Confederation of British Persons we might do things differently.

But never fear, the corrective is to hand.

Kemp:

But I suppose, in a way, the Treasury has to become the Confederation of British Persons to make sure this is so.

The elevated 'Confederation of British Persons', second only, it seems, to the House of Common British Persons across the road at Westminster, carries out its duties in this role by a process of elimination. At an early stage every single possible tax change is put down on a piece of paper, which David Norgrove, one of the Principals working on the Budget, obligingly showed us.

Norgrove:

I thought you might be interested to see a copy of the

document that's prepared at about that time and then constantly updated throughout the year, up to the Budget. It shows a huge number of minor and major possible tax changes, some of which are dropped at various stages and some of which are reinstated. Back here you can see that there's a list of various things that were eventually dropped, and they range from major changes in the Investment Income Surcharge to the treatment of the bonds issued by the African Development Bank.

And against most of the entries was a note about which minister, on what date, had authorised the proposal to be dropped. To do this intelligently, however, ministers need a vast amount of information about the effects of particular tax changes. So, to this end, in parallel with all the forecasting and lobbying, not to mention the peering at a far horizon in case a sudden change in the oil price is about to throw everything out, something called the Ready Reckoner is being put together. It's an instant guide to ministers, and others, on what will happen, for example, to the public spending borrowing requirement, the exchange rate and everything else if they cut income tax by ten per cent. But this is no ordinary reckoner; its arithmetic is heavily coloured by human judgement.

We were let into a meeting – one of several called to put it together. A delegation of economists from the Inland Revenue and Customs and Excise trooped in to meet their Treasury counterparts, in another of those unadorned committee rooms, essentially to see if they could agree. What would 2p on beer duty or 5p off the standard rate (these are notional examples) actually mean? The meeting was halfway between a seminar and a seance. Government economists have to cultivate this weird mixture of extreme meticulousness and a talent for blind stabs in the dark, assisted by well-remembered ghosts from the past. Half the time we were there was spent discussing beer, and those present seemed, rather charmingly, to have little more idea than anyone else why beer consumption had gone down, and what this should mean for the beer tax.[1] It all drove home a point Peter Middleton had made earlier.

Middleton:
I think the key to economic policy-making is to recognise

---

[1] Two months after this meeting took place the Chancellor in the Budget of 15 March 1983 put up beer tax by 1p a pint.

that you aren't ever going to be accurate because people's behaviour and responses are always changing, and the world's not getting any more certain. I don't think there's any prospect of greater accuracy. What you can do is to get a little bit surer about the direction in which the various measures you take are going to work but, as for the precise effect, you never really know.

But from the Inland Revenue, which collects the taxes and is much involved with this side of the Treasury's activity, one gets a more acute sense of how imperfect the techniques are. Sir Lawrence Airey, another former Treasury man, is the Chairman of the Revenue.

Airey:

I don't think they're in the dark about what will happen in the sense of the figures, the amounts of tax that will be paid by particular groups of people. What is more difficult is knowing how the particular people or companies will react to those circumstances, because what we do will depend not only on the tax change in question, but on a whole lot of other things. For example, companies in twelve months' time, when some tax change takes effect, will be facing all sorts of different circumstances in relation to foreign competition: there may have been changes in the exchange rate, there may have been changes in inflation, all of which will affect the decisions that they take. So it is very difficult sitting here now to know exactly what will happen in a year's time in relation to some company getting the benefit of a tax change.

Whether their estimates are right or wrong, the show must go on. As everyone never ceased to say, the Budget is the Chancellor's baby; all this activity by officials and economists is a preliminary to his judgement and his decisions. For Peter Kemp, the pace is hotting up:

Kemp:

At the end of the day, the decisions are the Chancellor's, of course, in conjunction with his ministerial colleagues and the Prime Minister, but in the build-up there is a very real and continuing dialogue. We are constantly in the Chancellor's room, throwing ideas around and looking at various mixes and packages.

There's no doubt that the pre-Budget weeks do put great pressure of work on a lot of officials. In the last week before the

March Budget Peter Kemp worked eighty hours, the weekend included. His central unit colleague, David Norgrove's workload reached its peak slightly earlier.

Norgrove:

You may find, for example, that there is a draft of a Budget speech to be got out at the same time as you're trying to pull together recommendations or analysis on the substantive issues that are being discussed in relation to the Budget. Those two things go together, and I think it's quite helpful that their preparation is, to some extent, concentrated in the same people. It helps to ensure that things are kept together and co-ordinated, but it does cause considerable pressure of work. In a way I feel at Budget time rather like a human word processor, only I have a biro and a pair of scissors and a stapler instead of an actual machine.

So, we wondered, is it proper to describe the amount of work as the preparation by officials of options, in great detail, with all their possible consequences, for ministers? Or is it more a dialogue between equals?

Norgrove:

I think it's more the former than the latter in that most options are considered, even if to be rejected fairly quickly, and then people begin to focus on the options which are the front-runners. There will be, of course, a dialogue about it. Officials will present papers to ministers which will then be discussed, generally with officials present. Ministers will listen to officials' views, but of course the decision on which options are going to be explored further is one that ministers take, not officials.

The Budget speech, of course, is where it all comes together. That public moment, the only one most people are aware of, is, you may be sure, given the fullest possible thought. The Chancellor has many scriptwriters composing draft after draft. For the Treasury, too, despite a tendency to loftiness, has the sense of Budget Day being its moment of greatest exposure. Peter Kemp, at the centre of the drafting effort, is as aware as any editor of the different audiences the speech has to satisfy.

Kemp:

It's got to be a number of things that it isn't always possible to be at the same time. It's got to be fairly clear and accurate because, even as it's being delivered, if somebody's saying something about the exchange rates or the markets, there are folk up in the City with their transistors on in their one hand and a computer print-out in the other, buying and selling sterling like mad, and so he has to be careful from that point of view. At the same time, he's got six hundred-odd MPs there in the House to listen to him, to barrack or cheer, as the case may be. He's now got, because of the activities of people like yourself, large numbers of motorists and housewives and the like, up and down the country, all listening to him, too.[1]

It's so much more of an occasion than a boring old White Paper.

Kemp:

It's not easy to get the right mixture of accuracy, listen-ableness, touch of wit – if we can get it in – and that sort of thing which goes to make an occasion. One might say, well, it doesn't much matter what the actual occasion is because, after all, it's what's in it that matters, and it wouldn't really matter very much if it was just printed and laid on MPs' doorsteps or issued as a monstrous press notice. I think that is to underrate the fact that there is still a certain amount of excitement and interest in this, and so a lot of attention is paid to the packaging, the speech. It's more than just wrapping: it is, I think, important in itself.

How much it has all been a collective Cabinet decision is, of course, a matter of some interest to vigilant constitutionalists. To Sir Geoffrey it's a rather subtle combination of the individual and the collective.

Howe:

The essential shape of the Budget, I think, must be the Chancellor's decision. In a sense, it's why he's in the job, and he lives in close proximity to all the factors that have to be taken into account. However, it is something on which one hopes to maintain a consultative relationship not just with one's Cabinet colleagues but with a much wider public audience, so that one's judgement can be seen to be well-founded. Not everybody will agree with it. I hope that in the Cabinet the position is generally supported – it usually is – but I'd like to carry support more widely than that. That's why I conduct a great deal of discussion between Budgets with my parliamentary colleagues on an almost

---

1 The 1983 Budget speech was broadcast live on BBC Radio 4 (and without interruption for comment on VHF), on Radio 2 and on BBC1 television and ITV.

continuous basis, and the shape of next year's Budget is the subject of debate from the moment this one finishes, as it were.

But could there be alterations, after the Cabinet has been told the final details?

Howe:

Well, the final disclosure is beyond the point of no return, so to speak, because one is determined by printing schedules and everything else.[1]

For Sir Douglas Wass, who retires at Easter, this year's Budget was his last. He's been an intimate witness to the making of scores of them, but the occasion still has not lost its excitement – nor the relief when it's over.

Wass:

It's a bit like boat-race night when one's an undergraduate. One has been working very hard, for perhaps two months, in conditions of secrecy which always add to the feeling of being a member of a corps, and therefore of a team. The Budget is the boat race; it is the day it all happens. It's all got to synchronise, things can go wrong, you're in a state of some nervousness and tension, and then it finally happens and the feeling of relief that it's all gone well without a hitch is tremendous. It's a bit like a sporting contest – in one sense, at any rate.

The man standing centre stage, however, is the Chancellor himself. He makes, in the end, a personal decision. And he brings to it, as Sir Geoffrey Howe reveals, that utter certainty that he is right, which may, in this uncertain world, be the politician's most arresting contribution to economic policy.

Howe:

In the end, the economic judgement is that for which the Chancellor is responsible, and one is very conscious of that at the time when it comes to be made. The judgement about the apparently very tough Budget in 1981 was my judgement, and the fact that it is now seen by most people as having laid the foundations for the progress that we've made

---

1 The Budget speech itself is not printed until it appears in *Hansard* and can be amended until the last minute, but the definitive proposals it contains are published in the *Financial Statement and Budget Report* which goes to press on the Saturday before the Budget. The Chancellor unveils the contents of the Budget to his Cabinet colleagues on the morning of his statement to the House of Commons on Tuesday.

since then and as an inescapably right judgement gives me
more encouragement now than it did in the anxious
moments when I was making it. But it really is essentially a
personal decision in the context of a welter of advice which
one takes from whatever quarter it comes.

At the beginning Geoffrey Howe made Budget Day sound like
theatre. To Douglas Wass it's more like a sporting contest.
What neither of these metaphors conceals, however, is that the
Budget really is the supreme moment of the Treasury's annual
existence. There is lobbying, of course, and vast quantities of
advice are received. At times the Cabinet gets in on the act,
although strictly at the Chancellor's convenience. The Prime
Minister, too, is obviously central. But when it comes to the
final decisions, other ministers often know little more than we
do until the day before. This is one moment for which the
Treasury does not have a single alibi.

The World Outside

First Broadcast: 20 March 1983

When the Treasury first occupied its present building in Whitehall, Britain was the greatest imperial power in the world. Now
the Empire has gone, and having lost it, we may also have lost
a role – but we have not entirely lost our currency. Industrially
Japan has left us far behind, but the pound sterling still matters
to far more people than the Japanese yen. The legacy of history
is a currency, an expertise and a global network which makes
the Treasury's overseas activity – almost entirely invisible to all
voters and most politicians – an essential part of its being. The
decline of Britain may have hugely diminished our diplomatic
power but has not, on the face of it, lowered our importance
in financial diplomacy to anything like the same extent. In a
sense, therefore, the Treasury is more powerful in this role than
it has any right to be. Pursuing it, it is energetic and far-reaching
and, as Geoff Littler, Second Permanent Secretary in charge
of overseas finance, indicates, it helps to keep the airlines in
business.

> *Littler*:
> We're a fairly thin staff. I think we're under a hundred for
> the entire overseas finance group. It's not so unusual that
> you get the situation I had in one week before Christmas
> where, on the international debt front, I had the Under
> Secretary in Paris, the Assistant Secretary in Basle, the Prin-
> cipal in Brussels, I myself was due to be in both Brussels
> and Luxembourg at the same time, and there was going to
> be a problem in holding a meeting with the Foreign Office
> that day to discuss what we should do next.

Or take Littler's personal diary, as he looked forward one day
in January 1983.

> *Littler*:
> I was in Riyadh last weekend, I shall be in Paris next
> weekend for three days, I come back and will have to go to
> Riyadh again probably, fit in a visit to Luxembourg and
> possibly one to Brussels before the end of this month, and
> then go to Brussels and Washington within the first ten days
> of the next month. It's fun but it's pretty tiring. I've said
> from time to time that the main qualification for this job is

to have a good metabolism, so that you can drink anything, eat anything, take any time change and any loss of sleep and not actually fall dead the next day.

Criss-crossing the world, Geoff Littler is a key fabricator of the infrastructure on which global economic policy-making is based, often preparing the way for the Chancellor of the Exchequer. On that level Treasury ministers of all major nations meet – as the Secretary of the US Treasury, Donald Regan, describes his encounters with the British Chancellor – as a kind of private freemasonry.

Regan:

We meet on the occasion of these regularly scheduled international meetings, such as the annual meeting of the IMF and the World Bank, and we meet at times at the interim meetings of those organisations, of the OECD and other such occasions, perhaps five or six more scheduled events. Then, as you know, there are a couple of meetings a year of the Group of Five finance ministers – that is, the ministers of Great Britain, France, Germany, Japan and the United States meet again on an unscheduled basis. Frankly, we try to avoid the Press at these meetings, they are purely meetings where we can discuss informally matters of considerable concern to us.

And a lot of phoning?

Regan:

Well, that's what the telephone was made for. Also, of course, we do have some correspondence, and we are in touch with each other through our subordinates.

Another key figure in the network is the chief civil servant in the French Treasury, Michel Camdessus. Describing his relationship with Geoff Littler and the rest of the British, he came up with a very apt image.

Camdessus:

I used to say that we are like tennis players. We play the same game, with the same partners, on different courts, sometimes in London, sometimes in Paris, from time to time in the United States, from time to time in Brussels. They are the same players playing the same game and having the same good relationship even when they play, playing tough but also, of course, fair.

The reason why tennis conjures up so much the right picture is that tennis between consenting partners is substantially concerned with keeping the ball in play. This is a lot of what economic diplomacy is about – substituting currency and interest rates for the tennis ball and computer link-ups for the court. We'll come later to the possible limitations of this activity as a contribution to the national interest, but not before observing that the British, seen from abroad, seem to be uncommonly good at it. One had heard that Treasury people didn't actually care much for all this foreign travel. At least, that's what Andrew Britton said. A spell abroad was part of the career pattern, but. . .

Britton:
There is also amongst Treasury officials a good deal of impatience with the diplomatic round, a feeling that too much foreign travel has something of a stultifying effect, that one of the most boring ways to pass your time is in drafting a communiqué, and that even cocktail parties become a bit of a bore when you've been to a few hundred of them.

Whether for this or any other reason, younger Treasury people do not go abroad as much as some people would like them to. A spell, for example, in Brussels is not regarded as a necessary part of their professional formation. And former Tory MP Christopher Tugendhat, the Budget Commissioner there, thinks it shows.

Tugendhat:
In matters relating to the IMF and to such problems as Third World debt and so forth, I have the impression that the Treasury does have a fairly worldwide approach. Where I think the criticism is justified is at a rather different level, and that is I wish very much that the Treasury would do more to give its rising stars, its bright young men and women, a chance to gain international experience. I find that, for instance, the Foreign Office, as one would expect, and the Ministry of Agriculture which is deeply involved in Community affairs, and some others in government as well, are very anxious to make sure that their chaps get jobs in the Commission or in other aspects of the Community, in order that they can derive the necessary experience which will then enable them to be better civil servants when they get home. I find the Treasury is extraordinarily reluctant to let people derive that sort of experience, and sometimes when it has let people go, as into the UK delegation here, no sooner have they mastered the job than they're whisked

home again. I would like to see a greater interchange between the British civil service and Community institutions in general, and I would particularly like to see it with regard to the Treasury.

And, according to Tugendhat's *chef de cabinet*, Paul Lever, a Foreign Office man, the natural horizon of a Treasury man is short – although times may be changing a little.

Lever:

They are not people, on the whole, who have been professionally brought up to worry about what Europe might look like in ten years time and what would be Britain's place in it, or even perhaps to think about the far-reaching international implications of the world that they inhabit. However, there is quite a difference now to the attitude of five or ten years ago when the international involvement of the Treasury was really rather limited. There was the Commonwealth Finance Ministers meeting, the IMF and the World Bank, but not a lot else. By contrast, Treasury ministers now are regularly involved in Community discussions, they are involved in other meetings which force them, at the ministerial level, to see other countries' economic problems in a way that they were not obliged to see them before, and this has an effect on the thinking of their officials. It is one thing for someone in the Treasury to read a telegram from the British Embassy in Bonn which sets out the constraints on German public expenditure and explains why it is that the Germans are likely to be rather bloody-minded over the British budget contribution at the next meeting. It is quite another matter when they get this direct from a German mouth – whether it's a German minister or a German official – and now increasingly they are getting things direct and they are obliged, therefore, to pay somewhat greater attention to the international dimension of what they do than was the case in the past.

On the other hand, the art of survival is a relevant talent within Whitehall as well. According to a Treasury man who did get to Brussels, its present representative at the UK delegation, Richard Butt, diplomacy, after a fashion, is very much a necessary skill.

Butt:

There's a good deal of diplomacy in Whitehall. The way the Whitehall village works requires that one deals with other departments the whole time, and you have to develop a certain skill there if you are going to be effective – indeed, if you are going to survive. In Brussels you're doing that for a larger part of the time and on a wider stage, but I don't think it's an essentially different ability. Indeed, even within departments these skills are necessary: departments aren't monolithic, there are different views that have to be reconciled. It's all the same process of finding consensus and agreement.

And from Washington Donald Regan wouldn't hear of the suggestion that our Treasury people might be described as a little inward-looking.

Regan:

Far from it, I think they are very much aware of what's going on in the world around us and, seen from my point of view, they're outward-looking rather than inward-looking. Mind you, each time I talk to them we are talking about external events, we don't normally discuss what's going on internally within Great Britain. But I would say that they are probably more skilled at knowing international problems than a majority of all of the other finance ministries.

A remarkable tribute – but capped by the Frenchman, of all people.

Camdessus:

I have to say very strongly – for it is my personal conviction – they are so able, so well informed, so experienced in all the fields of international co-operation, that they make a very positive contribution to each meeting. Thanks to their imagination they are very often the ones who make the negotiations successful, and they have an exceptional ability to discover which kind of solution can be made to work.

So Michael Camdessus, like Donald Regan, makes it clear enough that we're pretty good at the international game. Geoff Littler and his team sometimes sound like globe-trotting mechanics, heavily in demand to sort out the world economic machine: supple in negotiation, ingenious at finding solutions. But negotiation isn't always about that. Tennis isn't just about keeping the ball in play: a few winning smashes are also necessary. How good are the Treasury at winning? According to Geoff Littler, a great deal depends on the state of the domestic economy, by which test, surprisingly, Britain is better placed now than for a long time.

Littler:

I think there has been a longish period, for most of my career indeed, when we found in practice that our influence was minimal because our own domestic position was repeatedly in difficulty. Indeed, I remember a predecessor of mine, on one occasion when we were going through one of our periods of real difficulty, saying that the only respectable attitude for a UK official to take at an international meeting was to keep his head down, and if the Chairman did happen to ask for his opinion to say, 'Thank you very much, Mr Chairman. I agree with much of what my colleagues have said. Thank you', and stop. There was great embarrassment in taking part in discussions in which you wanted to say and recommend things which were manifestly not happening in our own economy. Over the last few years – and in some ways I date this from the turn-around in 1976 after the IMF experience – the position of the UK economy and its policies have been a little more respectable in the eyes of many other countries, and when one expresses an opinion it carries rather greater weight. I think the UK is now listened to with rather more respect than was the case ten years ago.

Based in Washington, the International Monetary Fund has become a kind of world temple of sound money and a reminder, as one walks its polyglot corridors, that finance is a truly international activity – even if, unlike at the United Nations, some (to wit, the founding fathers of the Fund) have more votes and more power than others. Sir Joseph Gold, an Englishman in Washington, has worked for the Fund since it began after the War, was its General Counsel for years and is still a consultant there.

Gold:

This is, after all, a financial organisation and the role of the United Kingdom in trade and payments of the world is still a very substantial one. In addition to which, of course, the financial services it renders throughout the City of London are extraordinarily important and maintain the prestige of the role of the United Kingdom in the Fund.

The real point about the Fund, however, is as a symbol – and occasionally an enforcer – of the truth that no modern economy, and no modern Treasury, exists in isolation. The Fund may not itself be a constraint on independent action but, as Richard Butt says, the constraints certainly exist.

Butt:

I think to say that any international organisation, whether it's the IMF or the European Community, is itself a constraint is a misconception. The constraint on Treasury policy working is outside in the real world; it is in the fact that other member states are pursuing other policies, that financial markets operate independently from the way that ministers want, that at any moment there are certain financial economic orthodoxies which prevail. There are periods of transition, but you also have periods when there is a very clear orthodoxy about these matters, and governments have to operate within this real international framework which is not laid down by monolithic IMFs or European Communities. It seems to me to be the myth that the IMF somehow controls things, or that the Community controls things and tells member governments what to do, but it's the wider environment that is providing the constraints, they don't flow directly from the international bodies. A lot of the time international bodies are merely the forum in which individual governments have to sort out amongst themselves how they're going to exist within these constraints and how they are going to partly shift or stretch them. The misconception arises because from time to time international organisations have to tell governments that they can't do a certain thing because they act as a spokesman for these constraints, so that people think that it's the international organisation which has actually created them, and I don't think that is normally the case.

Nonetheless, the European Community does look to many like a very great constraint, not least because of the enormous and highly-publicised efforts made by the present government to reduce Britain's net contribution to the Community budget: 'our money', which Mrs Thatcher has made famous in numerous attacks on the grasping continentals. This is also a classic instance where Treasury diplomacy has to be directed not merely at the world outside but within Whitehall itself, and especially at the Foreign Office. Over Europe, according to Paul Lever, the two departments have had clear differences.

Lever:

I think it's fair to say that traditionally the Treasury has been the one department of state that has been institutionally the least enthusiastic about British membership of the

Community. By this I don't mean that they've ever been opposed to it, but that they have inevitably tended to see the drawbacks, the pitfalls, the constraints, rather than excitement or the prospects.

An impression amply confirmed by Richard Butt.

Butt:

In my previous seven or eight years in the Treasury I'd never come into contact with the Community in any positive sense. Occasionally I'd been aware of it, usually – to be perfectly frank – I'd regarded it as a bit of a nuisance. It was something that required me to do last-minute briefing or bits of work which I felt I could have done without and I didn't see it in a particularly positive light.

One of the benefits Butt reckons he's gained from his spell in Brussels is that it's changed all that – though he retains a certain detachment from the Great European Dream.

Butt:

I think the fact that people like me come out to Brussels for three or four years will over time mean that we build up an increasingly large body of people in London who do have this first-hand experience, who do understand the ways of Brussels and who do understand what the whole thing is about. That isn't to say that we all go back fanatical converts to Europe. Most of us probably go back feeling that on balance it's a good thing, but also feeling that there is an awful lot of time spent, and indeed, wasted, on issues, that the whole thing is painfully slow, and that some of the things we get up to are absolute nonsense.

Within this nonsense, however, are the lessons of real life in a complicated, untidy world: and the impossibility of achieving anything other than by patient diplomacy, as at the meetings of finance ministers.

Butt:

Finance ministers meet about once a month – they are, in fact, required to meet with that degree of frequency by a decision which was taken by the Council of Ministers in 1974 – and the purpose of these meetings is to ensure that there is the highest possible degree of co-ordination between member states in pursuit of economic policy, and that their policies promote over time the convergence of the European economies. The process of which these monthly finance councils are the apex is essentially one of persuasion and co-ordination, and not one of the Commission proceeding by dictate and telling members states what to do. The council has a great underpinning, a great substructure, of committees, nearly all of which have as their *raison d'être* the sharing of information, the search for consensus between member states, both between finance ministers and between the central banks of the member states. It is essentially a process of talking rather than of acting or of execution.

At a strategic level this kind of institutional scepticism naturally gives the Treasury a different slant on these interminable European negotiations from that of the Foreign Office. As Geoff Littler describes it, Whitehall is not always a consensus society.

Littler:

We do have a lot of arguments and there is a running thread of difference about strategic objectives. The Treasury is concerned primarily, has to be concerned, with the economic and financial well-being of this country; the Foreign Office does tend to think much more in considerations of global strategy and a peaceful world. These concerns are not necessarily irreconcilable, but they do occasionally mean that we take different views of things and they simply have to be argued through. Should we make a tremendous fuss over a particular feature or would it be better to let that one by in order to preserve our good opinion and perhaps win the next two or three battles? I suppose there is a general tendency for the Treasury always to want to be tough and the Foreign Office always to want to wait for the next battle. That overstates it. It isn't very often that we have a serious argument and it's usually only at the tactical level.

Also, there's a fairly well-worn pattern, dividing up the two departments' spheres of interest.

Littler:

In fact the closeness may not be quite as great as you'd suppose, because we do have separate fields. The whole area of international discussion of macro-economic questions – the posture of the leading industrial countries, whether their policies are right, whether they should be trying to change the ways in which exchange rates are handled, and so on – is mostly carried on through the IMF and through the Group of Five[1] in their regular meetings, and the Foreign

---

1 The Group of Five consists of the USA, UK, Japan, France and West Germany.

Office are not part of that. We like to keep them informed, because it's part of their understanding of the world background and how it's developing, but they are pretty content to leave us in the lead of the whole of that range of subjects. Similarly, although we have a strong interest in some of their geopolitical problems – obvious examples are the politics of oil countries or the Middle East – and we do join them in many discussions on those, there they are clearly in the lead, and provided they keep us informed and give us the opportunity to comment there's no problem.

To smooth any disagreements out, moreover, there's always the Cabinet Office, where David Hancock sits at the centre of co-ordination.

Hancock:

The Community budget negotiations are necessarily a joint operation between the Foreign Office and the Treasury. There is a third department which also has a very strong say in it, and which is closely concerned because so much of the Community money is spent on agriculture, the Ministry of Agriculture. I spend a large part of my time chairing meetings or clearing briefs with those three departments.

Hancock is about to depart to head the Department of Education[1] – having, it's said, only just been pipped for the top job at the Treasury itself. From him you get the sense that, whatever their different nuances, all Whitehall has taken on board the authentic British sense of injured outrage.

Hancock:

There is no difference of view on the objective – we are all absolutely convinced that the Community arrangements as they stand, without correction, are unfair on the United Kingdom and that they must be corrected.

And Richard Butt is the first to acknowledge that this collective will is exercised, in the end, by a very tightly co-ordinated operation run from Hancock's office in London.

Butt:

There is extremely good machinery in London for resolving differences and working towards consensus and usually by the time an issue is being negotiated in Brussels we have a clear UK line and I'm not in any doubt about what I have

---

1 He became Permanent Secretary of the Department of Education and Science in May 1983.

to do. Very often I will have played a part in that process of building consensus, either by commenting from here or indeed by going to London and participating in meetings. A variety of interests – Foreign Office, Cabinet Office, Treasury and different parts of each of these organisations – will have been involved in formulating the line. In my two years here there have been very few occasions when I found myself having to take a line with which I was unhappy, and even in the case of the exceptions it's usually been a matter of nuance or the precise tactics. I may sometimes have felt it would have been slightly better to have done things in a slightly different way, but I've not been unhappy with the substance of any of the positions I've had to take. So I would stress that the co-ordinating machinery in London is good and thorough, and it isn't a question of one department vanquishing another, but rather of people talking things through and agreeing on the line to take.

Yet, in this subtle and delicate business, the bureaucrat abroad is in some ways given more individual power of decision – with more opportunities to commit an embarrassing error – than he is at home.

Butt:

When they go abroad, officials are meant to interact with their opposite numbers and not simply to parrot national positions. They are meant to take account of what other people say and to be flexible, and indeed, of course, that's the essence of negotiating, that one knows how far one can go in stretching and sometimes slightly exceeding one's instructions in order to reach an agreement. The more senior you are, the easier that becomes, and obviously if you're a minister you do that with greater freedom and greater authority, but even at my level it's a necessary skill. It means that one doesn't go simply as a delegate of one's member government to meetings and to negotiations, one goes with a certain amount of authority to take account of what other people are saying and to adapt policy accordingly. That's not very different of course from what happens in the domestic environment but it's more important when you're doing it externally. If I was controlling public expenditure and I made a concession to the Department of Health, and then got back to the Treasury and thought, 'My goodness me, I've made a mistake', I would ring them up and say, 'I'm sorry, you know, I realise that I gave away more than I should have done.' And I've made a fool of myself and lost a bit of credibility, but I can claw it back. But if one said this in an international meeting it's much more difficult to claw it back. I mean, you can do it but you do it at the cost of a certain loss of national prestige, and not just of prestige either but of good faith in negotiations.

When they reach the heights the topmost mandarins may even find themselves speaking, just like the minister himself, for their country.

Littler:

One does find oneself occasionally – I've had it twice within the last few months: once in Copenhagen at a meeting of Economic and Finance Ministers of the Community,[1] and recently in the Interim Committee which is chaired by the Chancellor[2] – actually having to sit in the seat of the Chancellor, with, as it were, his hat on, and speak for him. Now I keep fairly close to him in advance, and I hope I know what his mind is, but when I speak there I am speaking with full authority for the UK.

The European picture surely emphasises the most conspicuous single truth about the Treasury's approach to the wider world. It is, above all, pragmatic. Treasury men are problem solvers and doers of deals, limited all the time by the discipline, often very immediate and short-term, of money. The other capital where the Treasury presence is especially important is Washington. Here it has its man at the IMF, who, when we were there, was an extremely pukka mandarin called John Anson.[3]

Anson:

The principal reason why the Treasury needs a man in Washington is that the United Kingdom has the right to appoint a director to the Board of the World Bank. That is the principal function which I perform here and it is a Treasury function. In addition, it is convenient that the same person acts as economic minister in the Embassy, dealing with financial discussions with the United States Treasury and

---

1 The Copenhagen Summit was held on 3 and 4 December 1982.
2 The Interim Committee of the IMF is the policy-making Standing Committee of the IMF which comprises twenty-four leading finance ministers. Sir Geoffrey Howe was its Chairman from December 1982 to June 1983.
3 John Anson left Washington to become Deputy Secretary at the Treasury responsible for Industry in May 1983.

the economic reporting on the United States economy. Meanwhile Anson's colleague, Harry Walsh, keeps an eye on things of very practical interest, these so-called 'bilateral' issues.

Walsh:

In the case of the United States, for instance, we have a long-standing campaign with them about one of their policies, that is to say, unitary taxation, which is a form of taxation practised in individual American states, whereby they divide the tax revenues according to arbitrary criteria so that taxes are sometimes levied on income which does not necessarily take place within the country. It means that British companies can be subject to double taxation; we regard this as iniquitous and we're trying to get it changed.

You could hardly get closer to the nitty gritty. On a much grander scale, hard-headed pragmatism – occupying a quite different realm from the strategic imagination usually associated with the higher diplomacy – is at its most necessary in dealing with the most critical element of the world outside, the currency markets. During the lifetime of the first Thatcher government, the value of the pound rose and fell by more than fifty per cent and every percentage point can have an impact on trade and industry, not to mention future expectations for the currency itself. As Geoff Littler tells it, he sometimes lives in a world on the brink of falling out of control.

Littler:

I think there are many occasions when you begin to feel very troubled by what is happening and you wonder whether you have actually lost control or are about to lose control. We've been through a period of that kind very recently, just before Christmas; sterling was at eighty-five or so in our best measure of the effective exchange rate, having come down from about ninety-two over a month or more, and we didn't know whether it was going to go down further, and if so, how much further.[1] When that happens I would really challenge anybody to give a judgement on that situation which would be much more valid than that of

---

1 In the event it did fall further, after mid-January when Littler was interviewed. The pound sterling's international value measured against twenty-two other currencies was:

| December 1982 | 84.3 | February 1983 | 80.2 | April 1983 | 84.2 |
| January 1983 | 80.9 | March 1983 | 79.5 | | |

the next person with some knowledge of the field. You're at the mercy not only of şome unforeseen event but of the way people are going to interpret those events. You suddenly get some apparently strongly-based rumour that there might be an early election, and if the sentiment is built on that and you get a one-way market, you begin to wonder how competent you are to do anything about it. In the last resort the market is in charge on these occasions, and country after country, including ourselves with many others, have found that you can fight up to a point but not any further. Sometimes the market will go wild and go far beyond what it should, but the scale of what is happening is such that you have to let it have its way for quite some time.

To assist them in trying to keep the reins on this wayward beast, the Treasury calls on the services of the Bank of England. In fact, it's the Bank which is really responsible for implementing exchange-rate policy. The nexus between the Treasury and the Bank is influential across the range of economic management – the importance of monetary policy has given it a new primacy in recent years – but to encompass it adequately would have required a separate series of programmes. On markets, though, Bank people are very clear that this is where their particular expertise comes in. Eddy George is one of the executive directors there.

George:

It's certainly a very much bigger part of our function. We are present in both the gilt-edge market and the money market almost continuously, and dealing every day we have direct contact with the market continuously from hour to hour, sometimes from minute to minute.

But the director most concerned with currency markets is Anthony Loehnis, who gives just a glimpse of how the Treasury's own expertise merges, at times almost entirely, into the Bank's.

Loehnis:

We would certainly keep in reasonably close contact. It may be that when there's calm in the markets for a very long time one would go along and wouldn't have anything particular to discuss. But at any moment of turbulence in the markets, or moments where consideration might be given as to whether policy should be changed, there would be very

97

close dialogue and obviously I am then in touch with my opposite numbers a great deal. Indeed, the Bank as such is in touch with its opposite numbers at the level of the managers and those in the Foreign Exchange division several times every day.

The relationship between Treasury and Bank has been described as one of creative tension: which not all Bank people deny – although they see a clear line between the function of the two bodies.

George:

It's certainly creative in the sense that, in my particular area of monetary policy, there's no different axe to grind from one end of town to another. We do work together but our inputs are very different; at the Bank our input is very heavily a market-input, the Treasury's is much closer to the House of Commons and to political influence in a more continuous way than we are, and that influences their input. They're also, of course, more in the centre of a broader range of relevant issues. I think it's the coming together of those inputs which I would want to stress. Of course there are disagreements from time to time, but there are disagreements between different parts of the Bank and between different parts of the Treasury as well, so if by 'creative tension' you mean differences of view coming together from different directions, yes, I think I would agree, it is probably a good description.

A becoming modesty which is repeated, though with a glint of steel, at the other end of town.

Littler:

I wouldn't claim to have the immediate sense of what is happening in the market, which those who are in the dealing room of the Bank of England do have. But I'm on the phone to them regularly, as are one or two of my people, and by tracking what is happening over a period of time we acquire a recognition of the shape of things. I don't think any of us would trust our own judgement without talking to the Bank, but we would feel sufficiently well informed to challenge what they were saying occasionally, or at least, and more frequently, to carry the argument much deeper than some merely superficial comments that they might make.

Now these joint exercises in trouble-shooting are all very well. In fact, they're absolutely essential. Turbulent, unstable markets play havoc with everyone's prosperity. But a point we've so far only hinted at now comes fully into focus – and a question about currencies provides as good an illustration of it as any. This is the relative weight and time accorded in the Treasury to, on the one hand, perfecting its techniques for handling the world outside, and on the other developing a profound strategic view about handling the profound strategic problems embedded in the world economy. Take the intermittent negotiations over the European Monetary System, the EMS, the arrangement by which certain European currencies, led by the franc and the deutschmark, are yoked together, fixed and refixed relative to each other. Britain has never belonged, a fact which much distresses Christopher Tugendhat.

Tugendhat:

I very much regret that Britain didn't join the EMS at the outset and I very much regret that Britain is not a member now. The timing of when you join and how you join is, of course, always very important, but I do think that the doctrine of 'unripe time' has been invoked so often, and in so many different circumstances, that it doesn't really carry very much weight. The negative approach one ran into in London, or rather the pessimistic approach, was that this sort of thing can't work, it's all been tried so often before. Well, these things have been tried so often before and they often don't work, but this attitude compares unfavourably with the optimism, the willingness to try, the sort of frontier spirit that one found in some other capitals at that time. Of course, I accept that the pound is in some important respects different from other European currencies – because of oil – but there is an absolute British interest, in my view, in seeing more stable exchange rates in the world, and the EMS, the European Monetary System, is a good place to start.

What we discovered, however, were two quite suggestive details. First, although not a full member of the EMS, Britain puts the famous skills of its fast-footed Treasury experts at the service of Michel Camdessus and his colleagues.

Camdessus:

It is always very hard to negotiate the alignment because the interests of the countries around the table are so different. Thanks to their ability, thanks to the deep knowledge they have of all these currency matters and of the mechanism of our co-operation, they enter right into the debate, generally provide us with a good compromise, and contribute in a very effective manner to the final solutions.[1] But secondly, it emerged that the Treasury had tailored its advice to Labour and Conservative governments on the EMS in the ways best judged to line each government up behind the Treasury's own institutional hostility. One first-hand witness described – off the record, of course – how the same officials had first put the fear of God into the Callaghan government that the EMS would keep sterling too high for their domestic good; and then told the Thatcher Cabinet (which admittedly had its own instinctive dislike of EMS): 'If you join it, you realise the pound will have to fall'. Geoff Littler was one obvious source of clarification: *would* Labour be terrified of EMS keeping the pound too high – and the Tories of keeping it too low?

Littler:

Yes, but the thread running between both is that one is unhappy about a situation in which you are too closely bound. At times you may feel the need for the maximum flexibility – and I don't necessarily mean flexibility of movement in the market, but flexibility of decision about how to handle it.

You could call this, of itself, a strategic decision. But what perhaps it better illustrates is a congenital preference for keeping all the options open: maybe sensibly enough, but not in full consistency with the kind of grand plans for new global structures to hasten the recovery of the world economy, which a lot of people spend a lot of time talking about. As the Chancellor remarked in his 1983 Budget statement, 'the agenda for international discussion remains a full one'.[2]

Certainly, if John Anson is typical, deep, cool thought is less agreeable to the average Treasury official than the tireless impersonation of Action Man.

Anson:

I am never quite sure how much time one needs to think. Ideally, of course, one would spend an hour a day just reflecting on the world. On the other hand I think sometimes

---

1 At the moment when this programme was first broadcast, on the evening of Sunday 20 March, the finance ministers of the EEC meeting in Brussels were deadlocked in discussion on realigning currencies and the EMS was effectively suspended. A compromise alignment was eventually reached the following day, in a session chaired by Sir Geoffrey Howe.

2 *Official Report*, HC, Vol. 39, no. 79, col. 135, 15 March 1982.

one does one's work better when one is heavily pressed and one has to get on with each thing in turn as rapidly as possible.

Not all Treasury people are quite so reluctant to admit to long-term preoccupations. There has been something of a dispute at the top of the international economic community between those who do strive for a new long-term structure immediately, and those who think this could not be attempted until some more substantive convergence between the different national economies has been achieved. Geoff Littler thinks about structure even if he is unwilling, yet, to favour doing anything very dramatic about it.

Littler:

I think it remains the view of those in charge in Treasuries and Central Banks in most major industrial countries, and in the councils of the International Monetary Fund, that we still need to bring the economic performance of leading countries a little closer together, to make them a little more stable, before we can tackle the framework of management again. We are beginning to see the possibility of it. There has been a great moving together which was particularly marked in the Versailles Summit last year[1] when it was explicitly acknowledged that policies were moving together and that they should continue to move together, and that the five countries whose currencies make up the SDR basket[2] – that's the United States, Germany, Japan, France and ourselves – really must, under the surveillance of the IMF, be prepared to examine each other's policies and try to keep coherence and achieve stability among themselves. If that focal point in world financial arrangements could be established, then we would have the basis on which to develop much clearer long-term structure arrangements for management. But until we get out of the period of turbulence that we've had, and we're not quite home and dry by any means yet, I think it remains the case that we're almost bound to be afflicted by day-to-day problems and to have to concentrate on the unavoidable problem of reacting to them, rather than spending our time drawing up blueprints for the longer term.

---

1 The eighth world economic summit at Versailles, 4–6 June 1982.
2 The Special Drawing Rights on the IMF.

The truth is that, if one is looking for real strategic movement, it is, once again, the politicians who will have to provide it. Those notorious summit meetings are when this kind of advance is meant to be made. Maybe, as Roy Jenkins suggests, summits have limitations. He saw them as a participant when he was President of the European Commission.[1]

Jenkins:

They are *quite* important occasions which have a chance of helping the world economy to go somewhat better than it might otherwise do. They are not immensely important occasions. I attended four western economic summits[2] and I can only think of one which actually took any decisions, and that was the Tokyo one in 1979, which did take some decisions about energy targets which were more or less enforced throughout the member countries.

But they serve a useful purpose.

Jenkins:

Not because of the theatre aspect of the matter but because they make seven leaders, the most important leaders in the industrialised world, think more internationally for a short time beforehand and for a short time afterwards than they would otherwise do. It also slightly opens their minds as to how other people are thinking. It doesn't directly, dramatically affect their own policy decisions but it makes them debate these issues in a wider forum than would otherwise be the case. They all want to make quite a good impression before the coequals or semi-coequals throughout the world and it does orientate, perhaps briefly, their minds in a more open and international direction.

In this modest endeavour Treasury men are facilitators. They know how the machinery works and have a few ideas how it might work better. But they won't build you a new engine. They take the world as they find it. They'd say they have to: turbulent markets and intransigent nationalism cannot be wished out of existence. If it's a new international economic order you want, which many millions of people might say was overdue, especially if they're unemployed, don't go to the Treasury to find the blueprint. They would look at you slightly askance, and tell you that that's not what they're there for.

---

1 From 1977 to 1981.
2 London, May 1977; Bonn, July 1978; Tokyo, June 1979; Venice, June 1980.

The Powerhouse of Whitehall

First Broadcast: 27 March 1983

The Treasury, as we've discovered, has many human virtues. It's inhabited by men and women who are clever, quizzical, industrious and sometimes humorous. They combine intellectual scepticism and professional commitment in admirable measure. Socially, this is the home of the meritocracy, whose dexterous skills have outlived the waning of British power.

But – something has been missing. Manifold though these professional talents are, what exactly are they used for? We've concentrated on the method and the process of Treasury conduct, but behind it, indeed at the centre of all its purposes, stands the actual British economy – the real economy, as it's called: the business of making, buying and selling all the goods and services that constitute the daily life and determine the prosperity of the people of this country. The Treasury doesn't, or shouldn't, exist as a kind of super-abstraction. If the government machine has an impact on the economy the Treasury must surely be its powerhouse. Somewhere, as the accountants say, there's a bottom line, the final computation of profit and loss. And a fair test for the Treasury might be thought to relate, in the ultimate reckoning, to Britain's economic performance.

Beginning to analyse this proposition, however, one immediately finds that if one's talking about the hard practical grind of business and industry, the Treasury's direct contribution is distinctly limited. The people there, for a start, have little first-hand experience; a failure which, according to Sir Terence Beckett, Director-General of the CBI, goes nationwide, but which, all the same, surely presents a special problem for anyone charged with judging how to make the real economy work better.

Beckett:
I think this is an accusation which goes much broader than the Treasury. The country as a whole doesn't really know enough about business. I'm biased, of course, coming from where I do.[1] I believe that more attention should be paid

---

1 Sir Terence Beckett was Chairman of the Ford Motor Company 1976–80.

towards the creation of wealth. To that extent, I would certainly want a Treasury who spent some time in business in some way, and too few of them have.

To some people, the problem seems much deeper than that. Tony Benn, highly experienced as a Secretary of State for both Industry and Energy,[1] as well as being a socialist prophet, considers that the Treasury's gilded detachment, and the consequences which follow, stretch a lot wider than mere business.

Benn:

It's a macro-oriented department. It's very ignorant of industry, just as the City of London is very ignorant of industry, too. There are other problems as well, I'm not suggesting there aren't, but I would just put some of the responsibility on the fact that these extremely clever people, who believe themselves to be so, have never really understood the society whose economy they've been guiding.

This charge is not a new one, nor one of which the Treasury has been entirely unaware. But Michael Posner, who's been in and out as a special adviser for twenty years, believes that the problem has got, if anything, worse.

Posner:

It is true that the Treasury is out of touch. During the seventies there was a very considerable effort by successive ministers to bring the Treasury more fully into touch with things. When Mr Alan Lord, now at Dunlop, was a very senior Treasury official,[2] he had responsibility for industrial policy in a way which would have been unheard-of in the Treasury of a decade earlier. Now, I believe that the Treasury's interest in the grass-roots or in the dirty fingernail side of the economy has diminished since then.

Douglas Wass, the Permanent Secretary, rejects this, perhaps naturally. To listen to him you might think that Treasury waiting-rooms were filled with a never-ending stream of ambassadors from the real economy.

Wass:

We do, for instance, under my chairmanship have regular meetings with senior executives in business when we have informal exchanges about the state of business, the particular

---

1 Industry 1974–5; Energy 1975–9.
2 Alan Lord was Second Permanent Secretary (domestic economy) at the Treasury from 1975–7. He joined Dunlop in 1978 and has been managing director since 1980.

problems that confront it, and what steps, if any, the government could take to help, and I frequently ask my visitors what sort of a Budget they would want to help them improve their performance. Secondly, we do maintain very tight lines of communication with sponsor departments of the various industries in the Department of Transport, Department of Energy, Department of Trade, and the Department of Industry itself, of course. And from the experts in those departments, who are dealing directly with the industries they sponsor, we do get a lot of information about the problems of industry. If one takes, for instance, the petrochemical industry, I should think that there are quite a lot of people in the Treasury who could give you a very good unscripted account of what the problems of ICI are. I can give you any number of examples like that – it doesn't mean to say that we have the answers, but we may know what the government could do within the constraints of policy to help that industry. By and large, I think the Treasury has a considerable awareness of what the problems are at a sectoral level, not just in an aggregate way.

Also, the Treasury does send some of its own younger bloods out for spells of work seconded to the private sector – though, interestingly, this is much more often to merchant banks, assessing and doing deals with other people's money, than at the sharp end of risk-taking in industry itself. Alan Bailey, Deputy Secretary with special responsibility for industry,[1] is the nearest thing the Treasury has to an industrial specialist. And he seems to think the City in fact offers the right experience.

Bailey:

The Treasury's role is rather like that of a merchant bank, in that we don't need people who are involved in the day-to-day detail of industrial management, because the questions we have to consider are not those questions. It's much more like a banker having to look at applications from an industrial firm not needing to understand the details of the firm, but knowing where to go for specialist advice and knowing how to ask the right questions and see through the figures and get the financial details. So far as the central part of the Treasury's role is concerned, I do believe that

---

1 Alan Bailey was promoted Second Permanent Secretary in charge of public services in April 1983.

this is much more the kind of operation we are engaged on, and this is the kind of skill we need and can accumulate without having people actually seconded from industry in the Treasury.

Michael Posner, having noted that the industrial connection has waned, says, rather like Alan Bailey, that in any case it is less appropriate than the City connection. His only regret is that the traffic is mainly one-way.

Posner:

I don't think an industrial input into the Treasury is appropriate because the Treasury is necessarily concerned with high levels of abstraction of economic policy. Where you could argue for a stronger interchange is with the Bank of England and the City of London institutions generally. I'd assert, though, that to date the flow has been one-way only: bright Treasury officials, perhaps sometimes those who didn't reach the very highest ranks, went out and reached the very highest ranks in the City. The difficulty of getting young men to flow in the opposite direction is, of course, because Whitehall salaries, although far too high in the eyes of some of the Press, are, in fact, in City terms far too low to attract bright youngsters into Whitehall corridors.

To Terry Burns, the Chief Economic Adviser, almost any external experience is valuable for the very reason that it brings the embryonic mandarins into contact with a world unlike their own: an irrational one.

Burns:

I think there is a lot to be gained from people having spells in other organisations, whether it be in banks or in industry, to make them more aware of the functions that other people do and more aware of what life is like in other organisations where maybe people aren't always quite as reasonable as they are here.

The somewhat limited appetite – or perhaps time? – which younger Treasury people have for going outside is, however, not to be forgotten. It's as true on the public-spending side as with industry. Nick Sallnow-Smith, for example, the Principal in charge of monitoring expenditure on higher education, is evidently sparing in his ventures on to the campuses where the money is actually spent.

Sallnow-Smith:

I think it's something which is happening more often than

it used to. In January I'm going to Manchester to a course for university administrators, to whom I will speak about public spending and how the Treasury's role within it affects the resources that they receive. I also spent two days earlier on in this post at Bristol University and I'm about to move on,[1] but it's intended that my successor should go to a polytechnic. These visits aren't as frequent as one might like but we do try and fit them in.

Besides, there is always the stubborn illogicality of career patterns which is characteristic of the public service, and perhaps many other large organisations. Diana Seammen's spell outside was not immediately put to obvious use.

Seammen:

I spent two years at Warburgs, mostly in the corporate finance department doing mergers and acquisitions work. And I then spent three months with their associated bank in New York learning about the American financial system. When I came back I was put in charge of social security, which suggests that the direct benefit the Treasury expected to get was not very great.

The salient undertone of most of these comments from inside the Treasury – that outside experience is of only limited value – sometimes makes it sound as though they think it a positive disadvantage to have been to the coal-face. At this proposition Sir Frank Cooper, himself a king-mandarin, explodes with characteristic ridicule. He's just retired as Permanent Secretary at the Ministry of Defence, which probably has more contact with manufacturing industry than any other Whitehall department. He cannot accept that the Treasury must be a counting house in an ivory tower.

Cooper:

I would totally and utterly disagree with that. I do not actually see how anybody can stand aside from all the real problems of real life in a world which is changing very fast. They do their best, they all go and talk to industrialists and trade unions and go out to lunches and dinners, but this is no substitute for real-life experience. Because in the end I think everything should be run by people who have a real feel as to how it's run, who can sense when something's

---

1 Nick Sallnow-Smith left the Treasury in February 1983 for a two-year secondment to the City bankers, Manufacturers' Hanover Trust.

going wrong and sense when something's going right, and can also see an opportunity. But you do not get that sitting in a castle or a tower, or even going to a meeting and talking to industrialists and trade unionists and anybody else you want to talk to. There's no substitute for real experience, and there are very very few people in the Treasury who've had real experience.

Even inside government this view of the Treasury as detached from 'real experience' is one of the counts against it. It certainly used to be the case that the brightest and best of aspiring civil servants wanted to get into it. No longer so, according to Sir Kenneth Stowe, a Permanent Secretary at the DHSS. Is he *parti pris* as a beady-eyed outsider? He was certainly tart when asked whether, for the young high-flier, ambitious for power, the Treasury was still the place to be.

Stowe:

That depends on whether or not he's a well-informed high-flier or an ignorant one. If he were a well-informed high-flier, I think he might take the view that he would do well to work in an interesting department where he is coming hard up against the actuality of government, whether it is managing local offices which give out benefits or managing public authorities of various kinds. That is a real world that he would do well to learn a greal deal about.

And if he were a less well-informed high-flier, what might he be misled into thinking?

Stowe:

He might be misled into thinking that he would sit closer to what you earlier described as power by sitting in a central department where he would, in fact, be dealing at a relatively low level with all the issues in very general terms, in terms of great abstraction, and I think he would find that he would want for understanding of them.

Frank Cooper, one such spender, does make the Treasury sound as if it exists almost on another planet.

Cooper:

The people who work there are very clever. Intellectually they are extremely able, outstandingly so, there's no doubt about that. But they live in an isolated world and a different world from the rest of humanity. And until you change this, you're never really going to get an effective Treasury.

As usual, Sir Frank exaggerates to make a very valid point.

This question of effectiveness is highly relevant and highly contentious. Accepting, as Alan Bailey said, that the Treasury's tasks do not actually require its denizens to have fought at the front-line and lived to benefit from the experience, one must also record the rampant indignation of every Treasury official accused of living part of his or her time in the famous ivory tower. Bailey spoke for them all.

Bailey:

The ivory-tower analogy is really very far out of date. It isn't a comfortable ivory tower; it's not particularly comfortable and it's certainly not ivory.

And that's the way the hard men of Whitehall – the spenders, the people dealing with the nitty-gritty – plan to keep it. Sir Kenneth Stowe was formerly the Permanent Secretary in the Northern Ireland office.[1]

Stowe:

I have always made it my business to encourage senior Treasury people to come and see things for themselves. When I was in Northern Ireland I got Sir Anthony Rawlinson and his staff to come over and we flew them in a helicopter over Belfast, so that they would have an overview of that city. We exposed them to a serious discussion with the people responsible for security, commerce, commercial development and local government. Now that is not something that one invites an unwilling Treasury to do. On the contrary, it is something which, in my experience, my senior colleagues in the Treasury have been very anxious to do. They are very anxious to identify in the real world – the actual world of services and policies that departments like this exist to manage: what the problems are; where there are rough edges; where we ought to be doing better but aren't; where there are areas of potential development and problems to which we can't get serious solutions. I've never found any hesitation, any reluctance, on the part of the Treasury to expose itself to a greater knowledge of what the real problems are.

So clearly they are not monastic recluses. Let's try a different tack. Granted that the Treasury deals with everything at one remove, and that it can't honestly be blamed, for example, for the decline of the British car industry, what about its strategic

---

1 1979–81.

thinking? Here, surely, is suitable work for the Treasury, absolutely critical to long-term economic performance. How much time does the Treasury devote to it? Clive Priestley, head of the civil service efficiency unit outside the Treasury,[1] describes a problem which all of us can identify with.

Priestley:

I'm sure that any politician or official associated with the Treasury would tell you that the great bane of their lives is the necessity to survive until Friday night. I think that has been, and remains, a pernicious influence in Treasury working, as in the working of many departments.

There is one strand of thinking which wouldn't necessarily see this as pernicious at all and would claim that strategic thinking thrived on daily decision-making. David Norgrove lives in the middle of the latter.

Norgrove:

There is an immense pressure of work in many areas of the Treasury and that does sometimes lead to things not being done as well as they might be. But I rather doubt whether one would want to advocate the creation of a unit within the Treasury which would devote itself solely to strategic issues and spend time thinking about them, because it actually helps in strategic thinking to have the people doing it, at least to some extent, who are involved in the day-to-day pressures and the day-to-day activities and crises. That way they get a better deal for the major issues than if they were divorced and in some separate group.

The Chancellor himself, Sir Geoffrey Howe, obviously agrees.

Howe:

The day-to-day crisis management is not something that is with us everyday, I'm happy to say. Many so-called crises are reruns of pressures and tensions that are in the marketplace. So a great deal of thought is given to the longer-term questions. I think the problem about securing commitment to long-term policy changes comes back much more to the nature and shape of our society and its institutions. The parliamentary scene, the differences of so-called beliefs about how society should be run, makes one hesitate before one moves into major structural changes in the tax system,

---

1 Clive Priestley left the civil service in July 1983 to become Director of Special Projects at British Telecom.

for example, for fear that they might be overthrown at a later date.

To Roy Jenkins, who ran the Home Office before he took over as Chancellor,[1] the Treasury is a haven of calm, well suited to the tranquil contemplation of the longer term.

Jenkins:

The Treasury itself is a tiny department, in terms of numbers of people employed, compared with most other departments. It isn't very directly involved with the public and, therefore, in that sense it's well placed to do some strategic thinking. It's also not – or should not be – enormously affected by day-to-day crises which blow up in a totally unforeseen way. I once described the difference, in my view, between the climate of the Treasury and the Home Office as that of the Home Office being one of summer storms which come out of a clear sky, when something suddenly blows up which you know nothing about, you have no control over, which dominates the headlines of the newspapers and which gets people very excited. The Treasury climate, by contrast, is more like that of a long dark Arctic winter, maybe disagreeable, but almost totally predictable, and if the Treasury's being managed properly you've got a pretty good idea of the issues which you will be dealing with in two months' time, as well as today. This should give it a capacity – and I believe to a substantial extent it does – for taking a longer view than departments which have to deal with more immediate and unpredictable issues.

Geoffrey Howe's hesitation – over whether long-term changes would in fact survive – expresses one of the deepest problems about strategic thinking. Although Sir Terence Beckett, coming from the car industry originally, would like to see the Treasury behave more like the Ford Motor Company in thinking long-term, he conceded that this government has got closer to this ideal.

Beckett:

Where I come from we do have a Budget plan which is for the current year. Over and above that year we plan three years ahead, and for some of our things, like product planning and in some parts of our corporate planning, we plan

---

1 Roy Jenkins was Home Secretary 1965–7 and 1974–6, and Chancellor of the Exchequer 1967–70.

ten years ahead. We have to. Now in the last two or three years the government has made some progress on this; it has had a medium-term financial strategy, which is a four-year strategy, over and above the Budget. They are making a step in the right direction.

But the approach ought to apply far more widely and for far longer, precisely because governments keep changing.

Beckett:

If we're talking, for example, about a mix between atomic and coal in energy, you need to be planning that at least fifteen years ahead, and so I believe that we do need this longer planning base. Incidentally, other countries don't need it as urgently as we do, because there is substantial common ground between the main alternatives in their political system whereas ours really is highly precarious, and things do change in a very radical way in a very short space of time.

Which is where, presumably, the continuing 'official' Treasury ought to come in – and where Labour politicians most suspicious of Whitehall think it does come in – as the purveyor of a kind of unvarying orthodoxy which is proof against political change. However, it really is with strategy that the political lead is important. Geoffrey Howe spoke about making changes that would not be overthrown. His opposite number, Peter Shore, has his own ideas of ways of achieving the same thing: his own medium-term plan, but also Labour's long-held conviction, that the Treasury is not the place to drive forward an industrial strategy for the real economy. Having created the Department of Economic Affairs for this purpose, which he led for two years until its demise in 1969, Labour would now try again.

Shore:

Serious medium-term planning is, I believe, necessary and it's crucial for industry. I would very much like to see a strong Department of Planning and Industry. I think that's the title we've given to it.[1] The job would be to take an ongoing, four- to five-year view of the economy and above all of industry, and would therefore be able to stand up for industry against all the short-term pressures that come from

---

1 A joint Labour Party–TUC statement, *Economic Planning and Industrial Democracy*, published in 1982 and subsequently incorporated in Labour's 1983 general election manifesto, included a provision to create a new Department of Economic and Industrial Planning.

events and from the competition of colleagues and so on. You could call this an example of the politician's essential optimism, that making changes in structures will necessarily produce better results. It also represents, quite clearly, an indictment of the Treasury and its ultimate capacity to nurture the real economy. Should we, therefore, be blaming these, the topmost mandarins, for so much that has plainly gone wrong?

Some people are quite adamant. Tony Benn, for example, offers a verdict which unequivocally places the Treasury as the fount of all error.

Benn:
It has a lot of international links and is the pipe through which a lot of powerful forces in the world express themselves to the Chancellor rather than directly to the Cabinet. It has its own policy. I suppose you could argue that the economic failure of Britain since the war could be attributed primarily to the Treasury because they've always been in power.

Before exploring the Treasury's responsibility for post-war failures, this easy talk about its power needs to be sorted out. As we shall see, Treasury people themselves are exceedingly ambivalent about admitting to the possession of any real power at all. Tony Benn is the best exponent of the contrary view. So how did he define Treasury power?

Benn:
It has a lot of influence: first of all because finance touches all policy – everything can be turned into public-expenditure targets; secondly because financial crisis is the most difficult thing politically for any government to handle; thirdly because the Prime Minister is First Lord of the Treasury and therefore supports the Chancellor.

It also holds many people's careers in the palm of its hand.

Benn:
Its influence extends to other departments because, even though the Treasury is no longer responsible for civil service promotions, any civil servant who gets across the Treasury would certainly be blacklisted for future promotion in Whitehall.

Treasury power could theoretically be reduced if the Prime Minister challenged it.

Benn:
Where you get a Prime Minister who is out of sympathy

with Treasury policy, then I would imagine there would be a great deal of difficulty. It would be possible, up to a point, to influence and delay the policy from No. 10. But all the Cabinets I've been in[1] have been Cabinets where the Prime Minister has really been in line with Treasury thinking, and looking back I think that's been one of the reasons why these Cabinets haven't achieved the objectives upon which they were elected.

But at its most ruthless the Treasury could control not merely decisions but the facts on which they were based.

Benn:

When I had my officials in to look at energy forecasting, they gave me the forecast and there was this great energy gap. It was intended to be filled by nuclear power, but they didn't want to tell me that and so I said, 'Well, let's look at the assumptions'. When I asked for them I found that all hell broke loose in my department because my officials had been forced to put in assumptions about rates of growth and inflation and so on, which had come from the Treasury and which they didn't necessarily agree with. I then realised that the Treasury had written our entire energy forecast, because if you assume such and such rate of growth and such and such rate of economic activity and such and such inflation, then actually as a minister I was looking at the out-turn of a Treasury forecast, or to put it another way, a set of Treasury assumptions presented as a forecast. That is the way in which people who are working on an inside track can to some extent, if ministers are prepared to go along with it – which in some cases they are, I'm afraid – set the framework of argument within which decisions are taken and, regardless of whether the minister takes option A or B, he isn't really challenging the basic assumptions which have been put in by the Treasury.

To round off this menacing picture, one of Tony Benn's protégés, Labour MP Michael Meacher, sees the Treasury as the nerve-centre of a national and international network.

Meacher:

The other very significant power of the Treasury lies in its contacts with outside organisations. Not only, of course, is

---

1 Tony Benn served in the Wilson Cabinets of 1964–70 and 1974–6 and the Callaghan Cabinet of 1976–9. He was Minister of Technology 1966–70, Secretary of State for Industry 1974–5, and for Energy 1975–9.

it the channel through which the City, the CBI and leading directors of major companies feed much of their advice about economic policy, and from which the briefs going to Treasury ministers are constructed, but it also has very close, literally daily, contact with other organisations. Internally there's the Bank of England, where they control the very key decisions taken almost hourly; externally there's the IMF, the EEC, OECD, the Group of Five and the Group of Ten – the key nations running the western economies. Now, that is done at divisional level within the Treasury, and there is certainly an enormous concentration of power there, over which ministers can do no more than give a general steer.

Turn to the civil servants, however, and the story begins to sound quite different: and to an extent which goes beyond the natural and deceptive diffidence of all people who are charged with the possession of power. Sir Frank Cooper actually doesn't deny that the Treasury is powerful – but this, he says, is entirely within the canons of constitutional propriety.

Cooper:

The knight mandarins of the Treasury are less in charge of the Treasury than any Permanent Secretary is of any other department, because quite frankly, whichever government is elected, it's the ministers in the Treasury who call the shots.

Sir Frank may be more blunt that some of his colleagues, but essentially they all see their power, if they have it, as being shackled by ministers on the one hand and by economic reality on the other. Sir Kenneth Stowe – echoing his predecessor, Sir Patrick Nairne, in *No, Minister*[1] – concedes that power all over Whitehall has a lot to do with information.

Stowe:

The power of the Treasury, like the power of any other government department, derives from its ministers and the central position which they occupy in the Cabinet. Decisions which the Cabinet takes relating to this department occur every year, as with any other major spending department, when they consider the public expenditure programmes. That is where all that we've been saying hitherto comes into focus. Because, if we have not satisfied the Treasury – and

---

[1] 'I do think that power can often lie, in theory, in the way in which civil servants can manipulate information.' Sir Patrick Nairne, *op. cit.* p. 27.

if the Treasury haven't satisfied themselves – that we should be allocated the resources that we've said should be deployed as set out in our public expenditure programmes, then neither of us will have satisfied the Chancellor, and you'll have defective decision-making at the centre of government. Now, the Treasury's power rests upon their getting the facts before the ministers – all the facts, not some of them. It's in our interest to ensure that they get them and that they have a full understanding of them. Now, if that is power, well yes, they have that sort of power and so they should. But equally, we have the power of being able to present to our ministers the same agreed facts, and if we've done the job properly, then there should be a very substantial area of common ground between the Treasury and the department, when the essential decisions come to be taken.

Still more drily, Douglas Wass picks apart the Bennite assumptions.

Wass:

Well, what is power? What power, over what or over whom? Certainly ministers confer power on to officials and most of the power we have to do things is derived from ministers, just as ministers derive their power either from statute or prerogative. It's very limited power. In the Treasury we have the power to say 'no' to certain expenditures, but if our 'no' is a capricious or perverse 'no' it will be challenged by the person to whom we say 'no', making an appeal to higher authority, and ultimately the appeal will go to the Cabinet and will be settled there. So the Treasury has no ultimate power to say 'no' which is not subject to appeal. That in itself is salutary. It makes the exercise of that power to say 'no' a much less arbitrary one than it would otherwise be, and a much more sensitive one than it would otherwise be. So I think one's got to recognise that though we are authorised – and that's another way of saying we have the power to do 'x', to approve expenditure or not to approve it – we're doing it within a framework which is conferred on us and subject to appeal and review by higher authority. That makes a lot of us feel that we don't have much power.

Nor, according to David Hancock,[1] a Treasury man in the

---

1 David Hancock was Deputy Secretary at the Cabinet Office 1982–3. He became Permanent Secretary at the Department of Education and Science in May 1983.

Cabinet Office, does the place even have the control over Whitehall careers that it once had.

Hancock:

So far as the Treasury's position as an institution is concerned, you must remember that the reputation for power derived from a time when, in addition to his present functions, the Permanent Secretary of the Treasury was also the sole head of the civil service and controlled senior appointments, advising the Prime Minister about the appointment of Permanent Secretaries. To that extent it was a more powerful institution. But the split between the Head of the Treasury, as we now know it, and the Head of the Civil Service, as it existed right up until the abolition of the Civil Service Department,[1] was made before I joined the Treasury, so it hasn't been like that for a very long time.

As we've said, you'd expect the mandarins to talk in this self-deprecating way. And it's not entirely believable. Within these rigorous procedures and this obeisance before inescapable reality, personal judgement can always be exercised; and Whitehall has its own networks of intense power politics. All the same, it is interesting to find, at perhaps the most extreme opposite end of the spectrum from Tony Benn, his Labour ministerial colleague, Peter Shore, who doesn't even seem to think that ministers, let alone civil servants, have much power.

Shore:

The idea that the Treasury is, as it were, the master of government is too cynical. What ultimately gives the Treasury its authority is the facts of the situation, rather than the arguments and weight of the ministers themselves.

Still, however complex the truth about power, the question of responsibility cannot be allowed to get lost in a convenient sea of confusion. Do mistakes get made? Should officials care about them? Has there been one Big Mistake in the management of our ailing economy? David Hancock expresses the loftiest view, which he might call simply pragmatic: error is rarely obvious, it may take years to prove, and life's too short to bother much about it.

---

1 The Civil Service Department, whose first Permanent Secretary was Sir William Armstrong, was created in 1968. It was abolished in 1982 and its functions were split between the Treasury, the Management and Personnel Office, and the Cabinet Office. The Secretary to the Cabinet now has sole responsibility for advising the Prime Minister on senior appointments.

Hancock:

When it is clear that something has gone wrong in economic policy-making, the mistake will have happened some years before. This is an important point. By the time it is clearly agreed that such a thing was a mistake, it will have been analysed over and over again, policy will have moved on, and by that time the people in the team are dealing with current problems, not rerunning history. I think that is why these feelings of remorse which you might expect are not very apparent, because everyone is engaged in a very lively debate about what to do next and not feeling guilty about something that happened in the past. I think myself that this is a perfectly healthy mental attitude. It would not be a good thing to have a government department staffed by people who were constantly feeling guilty about things, not all of which they could have influenced.

We did not find much self-confessed guilt, on matters either small or large, although Diana Seammen did admit to one mistake.

Seammen:

I once gave the entire confidential briefing on a Banking Bill to the opposition when it was going through committee, though in fact that turned out not to matter very much.[1] Whether you can make an irretrievable error or not is an interesting question. I don't know. It would depend, I suppose, on just how much you really wanted to run an area yourself and deliberately kept others out of it. In those circumstances I suspect that you probably could make an irretrievable error.

Interestingly, it was parliamentary performance which others regarded as most exposing them to the possibility of error: the

---

1 The Banking Act 1979. Later we asked Diana Seammen to elaborate on this incident: 'What happened was that we had prepared very substantial briefing on each of the clauses of the Bill (as is normal practice) for the Minister, who was Denzil Davies. I inadvertently left my copy of this document in the Committee Room, where it was later picked up by Ian Stewart who was leading for the Opposition. A good deal of hilarity ensued at the beginning of the next Committee Session, as I wondered whether to hand in my resignation on the spot or simply wait until after the Committee had finished. In fact, there was nothing in the briefing which we would not have been happy for the Minister to use during the debates, so no harm was done. Following this debacle we distributed the document to all members of the Committee and the quality of debate was probably higher as a result. Denzil Davies took it all extraordinarily well.'

one moment when they ventured out to defend the Treasury or explain policy in the glare of publicity. Nicholas Monck, Under Secretary in Home Finance.

Monck:

You could put your foot in it quite badly in giving evidence to a select committee. I mention that because it is a relatively new thing and now we all have to give evidence, every word of which is recorded and you can quite easily make a mistake. The other bigger thing which could go wrong is if you were consulted on what to do about something happening in the market and, as can occur, it had to be decided in five minutes, you couldn't actually get to a minister in that time, and you'd have to say 'yes' or 'no.' Then there could be great recrimination about it afterwards.

But had this ever happened to him? He did not prevaricate.

Monck:

No.

A monosyllable rather more grandly spelled out by David Hancock.

Hancock:

I think if it was recognised as being irretrievable, the mistake would be made because I'd obeyed my ministers. I don't wish to be facetious in saying that. It's just that if it is of that order of importance, then the decision-making processes demand that the submission is made to ministers, and it is they who take the decision. It is our duty to make sure that we don't take decisions which have serious consequences without referring to ministers, and we are therefore very careful to do that. I cannot think of an example of someone failing to recognise a disaster before it happened.

But what about disasters after they've occurred? Some people describe the whole economy as a disaster area. The Treasury takes a more philosophic view, not least about its own culpability. It doubts whether the story is one of failure anyway. Although Douglas Wass can think of things he personally got wrong, there's little he would nail on the Treasury as a whole.

Wass:

I would say that our performance in relative terms, in terms of economic growth, in terms of productivity and so on, has been a good deal poorer than that of our continental neighbours and Japan. In terms of our historical performance, of course, it is better than we had, for instance, over a large part of our economic history. Whether I personally feel responsible, I suppose I could – and it would be very immodest of me to pretend that I couldn't – identify particular analyses and policy recommendations I had made which with hindsight I regret, or perhaps with hindsight I would have made differently. I think that's not the same thing as saying that I feel personally responsible for our performance having been less good in terms of economic growth than France. I think what has contributed to the differential performance of the UK vis à vis its continental neighbours is a multiplicity of factors which are far too numerous to go into in a discussion like this.

In any case, as Wass's heir apparent, Peter Middleton, says, from the perspective afforded to an official much more easily than to a politician, judging failure is very much a matter of taking the long view.

Middleton:

The problems involved in getting the British economy up to the world average rate of output are very great and probably long-term. So this is an area in which I don't think one could look for instant success, and you can do very silly things by actually trying for that. What one wants to feel is that one is getting the economy on a long-term course which will achieve that objective. As of now, of course, we are going at the same rate as the rest of the world, but that's no very great comfort when the rest of the world's going at zero.[1] I think the next ten or twenty years will tell but I wouldn't admit to any feeling of failure so far. Life is a struggle and I don't think that there's any way in which the Treasury as such can produce a successful economy. You can produce conditions in which a successful economy can take place, but a successful economy takes a good deal more than that and it takes a good deal of time.

And even these conditions may be only marginally affected by anything at all done at the Treasury. Rachel Lomax, Senior Economic Adviser.

Lomax:

Officials must be implicated to some extent in policy mistakes which have been made over the last twenty-five

---

1 In the last quarter of 1982 the OECD National Accounts gave the UK economic growth rate (as compared with the last quarter of 1981) as +2.7%; that of the USA −0.9%; that of West Germany −1.9%; and that of Japan +3.7%.

years. But I think the extent to which policy mistakes have actually contributed to the problems of the British economy is very debatable. There is a limit to what you can do at the margin by economic policy, both the damage and the good, and in that sense I think the damage that the Treasury can be said to have done is fairly limited.

Besides, it hasn't been all damage. Sir Anthony Rawlinson.

Rawlinson:

Though it is perfectly true that the British economy has not been as successful as probably all of us would wish, and as some other economies have been, it hasn't been all that bad either. However, there are certainly many features of it, not least the unemployment at present, which are extremely worrying. But do officials who work in the Treasury feel some responsibility for this? Answer, I think, yes. I don't myself believe that the Treasury or any other department, or any particular set of ministers or governments, are wholly responsible for these things, but I think they have probably contributed something and I shouldn't wish to exonerate Treasury officials from a share in this. But equally, one can perhaps claim some credit for things that have gone right, and some things have gone right, not least on the public expenditure side.

And there are more cynical conclusions, perhaps especially noticeable to a recent escapee from the place, Andrew Britton.

Britton:

I don't think that the Treasury itself feels a sense of failure. It probably feels a sense of frustration but on the whole officials probably go around with the thought in the back of their minds, 'If only they'd done what I told them to, it would have been all right'. They may be wrong in feeling like this, but if you ask how they maintain their self-confidence in the face of the appalling mess of the British economy, I think it's because, never having actually taken decisions, they are always able to satisfy themselves that, if they had taken the decisions, they would have taken the right ones.

Not everyone at the Treasury is quite like that! We came to the conclusion that the varied reactions of Treasury people to the condition of Britain was a matter of personal temperament as much as anything. Some protect themselves by cool detachment. Others, like Geoff Littler, the Second Permanent Secretary in charge of overseas finance, sound more passionately engaged.

Littler:

I think, in these matters, none of us who are really in the centre of important decisions feel we can get away with just sheltering behind the minister and the fact that it's his decisions. Even if you are plain overruled in your advice, you remain worried by the question, 'Was it your personal failure in not putting that advice sufficiently strongly, competently, persuasively?' And you can't escape this responsibility.

This poses a particular problem at the moment.

Littler:

We have opted for a form of policy which is achieving the important results of reducing the rate of inflation and bringing down interest rates again and providing, I believe, the basis for improved performance in the future. It is coupled with quite devastating figures for unemployment.[1] One can't just draw back and say, 'That's not my problem'. I don't want to suggest that I lose sleep all the time over the entire social scene, but when we're actually working on and thinking about these policies I think we all, in a sense, put ourselves in the position of the minister. If you don't, you're not going to give the right kind of advice.

But this, in the end, struck us as the exception. Most Treasury officials are unable to let themselves feel like that; are quite happy, these days, to be technicians. The palmy days, when the official Treasury knew what it thought and fought to the death against a minister's right to contradict it, have utterly gone – and with them, according to Andrew Britton, some of the commitment.

Britton:

Over the last few years the strategic decisions about policy have not been taken by Treasury officials, and Treasury officials have become accustomed to not taking them. For that reason, I think they've had less incentive to crystallise their ideas to the point where there could be a corporate Treasury view which one could articulate. There has been a tendency to take strategic decisions for granted and to think

---

1 In February 1983 the UK rate of inflation was 5.3%, the base interest rate was 11.0% and the seasonally adjusted rate of unemployment was 12.6%.

rather about the means of implementing the government's policy, whilst keeping a great deal of mental reservation and intellectual scepticism about whether the whole thing is going to work. But rather than trying to erect an intellectual alternative there has been a tendency to live rather from hand to mouth, thinking of ways in which the policy could be made to work and, if necessary, adapted a bit at the margins to make it more workable. There was a period when there was a Treasury view and the self-confidence was associated with it, and the self-confidence has survived the passing of the Treasury view. People, having developed this self-confidence, have somehow maintained it, despite the intellectual vacuum round which it is now, in effect, built.

And to confirm the new, much more restricted ambition to which this self-confidence is directed, listen to two of the younger high-fliers – the new generation of embryo-mandarins. First, the Treasury's man in Brussels, Richard Butt.

Butt:

There is an interesting question as to why we haven't all had nervous breakdowns and collapsed into neurotic heaps because the economy doesn't seem to respond to our policies. I suppose part of the answer may be – certainly I think it's the view of the present government – that failures hitherto have been because the Treasury has tried to do too much, because it has claimed greater potential powers and ability to put the economy right than was sensible.

A modesty endorsed with even more disarming clarity by the Treasury man in Washington, Harry Walsh.

Walsh:

When a government comes in with an *idée fixe*, there is nothing that any civil servant can do if the government is determined enough to implement it. The minister will simply request you to do something, you may say that this has certain disadvantages, but at the end of the day you must implement it. The question then amounts to who is more skilful at implementing that *idée fixe*: someone who knows how to operate policy or someone who does not.

But what Harry Walsh went on to say encapsulated a good many doubts in the Treasury about whether any particular policy, let alone its policy of the moment, was necessarily the right one, or whether any other policy would have forestalled the relative failure of the British economy.

Walsh:

Well, I think the key word there is 'relative' failure. I think that there has been at least some absolute growth in the British economy over those twenty years, and that the conditions of life for most British people have in fact improved. At the same time, it seems to me that relative failure is not something with which we should be content and it is something we should try to improve on. The problem is that no one quite knows how to do it. If there was a plan for doing this I'm sure it would have been discovered by now. But it just so happens, I think, that the particular constellation of factors in the British economy has led to relatively low growth in productivity and a very modest improvement in living standards compared with other countries in Europe. It seems to me that we should aim at least to be in the higher band of countries in Europe, as regards wealth, and not in the lower band. It's easy to criticise those responsible for economic policy, but it's much harder to tell them what they should do in order to get the conditions right for improved growth. I have never seen any solution for the British economy that could be successful, certainly on the basis that the activities of the officials responsible for running the policies could be improved. The officials themselves can implement policies smoothly or unsmoothly, stupidly or wisely, but in so far as we've had policies of various types down the years, I don't think that officials running them more smoothly would have made them any more successful.

For such disclaimers Treasury officials have been called some rude names by the zealots of modern conservatism: almost as damning in their way as the anathemas handed down by Tony Benn. Their pessimism and defeatism, it's been said by people quite close to the Prime Minister,[1] are all that stand between the Thatcher government and the uplands of a golden future. From this stigma, however, the first person who comes rushing to rescue them is the Tories' own appointee, the young and unquestionably zealous Chief Economic Adviser at the Treasury, Terry Burns.

---

1 Sir John Hoskyns, head of the policy unit at 10 Downing Street 1979–82, said at the annual dinner of the Institute for Fiscal Studies on 12 October 1982, 'For twenty-five years failure has been built into the country's system of government. Exhausted ministers, advised by deeply pessimistic civil servants who do not believe the country can be saved from decline, have blocked the development of a strategy for recovery.'

Burns:

The British economy has been a very difficult beast. It has shown itself very slow to change, it is very slow to adjust; it does move under pressure, but it does it a great deal more sluggishly than many economies. We have had a number of shocks and unfortunately we're living in a world where a substantial amount of change is needed. Within that the Treasury, of course, is involved in trying to use the best knowledge that is available about the way the economy works, what the pressures are, and the kinds of results that are going to come from different policies. I'd have thought that, by and large, the way in which the Treasury has conducted itself and the views that it's taken have tended to be very much in line with the broad thrust of academic opinion within the economics profession at the time that it was doing it. So, to the extent that there have been major errors of perception or analysis at different stages, which subsequently people have changed their views about, then the Treasury will, almost certainly, have shared in them at the time. But I think it's very difficult to identify any particular responsibility which lies within this building.

The accusation that officials are pessimists and culpably defeatist manages, in fact, substantially to misunderstand the nature of the civil servant, and more important, the nature of the British economy. And it's one to which Peter Middleton reacted with some resentment.

Middleton:

No, I don't feel like a defeatist or a pessimist, and I don't see why I should either. I think one has to keep on pursuing policies which increase efficiency – which is the single most important thing in the economy – with a macro-economic background which best promotes that, given the policies of the government of the day. If you succeed in taking steps along that road, by and large you can't be doing anything which harms the British economy, and the chances are that you'll be doing things which do it a great deal of good. But it is an operation which can't totally be conducted by Treasury officials, it would be ridiculous to say that it could. It's a question of national attitudes and of the whole way the economy works, and that's a process which everybody's involved in.

Besides, calling mandarins pessimists, says Douglas Wass, is

125

criticising them for not being magicians of alchemy.

Wass:

It's a criticism I've heard. I don't accept it. It's the criticism of the philosopher who cannot transmute base metals into gold. I regard myself and my colleagues as being realists, and not unoptimistic realists. And as for myself personally – we're all different of course – I feel that I am an optimist. I don't take a pessimistic view of most of the problems that come my way. Perhaps by nature I am something of an optimist, but at heart I am a realist. I don't let my optimism carry me away.

Sir Douglas is about to carry himself away into retirement to be succeeded by Peter Middleton, who's been picked partly because he's a bit more gung-ho – a bit more, dare one say it, like a politician. Whether the Treasury will change much is another matter. It will continue to be a clubbable place, full of hard work and personal parsimony. No free lunches there; and not many power-hungry conspirators either.

Power, in fact, is not, as we've discovered, its most conspicuous attribute at all. Clearly, when backed to the hilt by the politicians, it exerts power over the rest of Whitehall on public spending limits. But its power over the economy is much diminished by the considerable self-doubt which has obliterated the certainties of old. Treasury men, even the hairy ones, have great sophistication and admirable finesse. But it is another part of their honesty to wonder from time to time, perhaps now more than ever before, whether, whatever they do, they can make all that much difference to the real economy. Will Britain become a richer or a poorer place to live? That, as they've repeatedly said to us, is determined by factors which, from their corner of Whitehall, they can barely reach.

Postscript

After the programmes had gone out, and the Treasury had been duly exposed to the world, we thought it worth trying to find out how those inside had taken it. A few views from further afield also seemed worth collecting. After all, we had not employed any expert advisers ourselves, or any of those 'consultants' who occasionally grace the credits at the end of television investigations of private worlds and expert subjects. If the programmes were to stand the passage of time in print, it was important to find out how accurate our picture was. Curiosity, if nothing else, drove us back on the circuit: even though, courtesy being what it is, even in the Treasury, we knew we might not get the unvarnished truth about official reactions.

One contributor at least did not like the series. 'I felt it was superficial. Too bitty. What we would describe as doing a salami job. You chose a quotation to illustrate the point you wanted to make, but the question really is whether these tiny snippets, which may prove the point, are representative of the situation in depth. The outside listeners might have got a better impression if fewer subjects had been covered in depth, rather than so many facets in a rather shallow way.'

But other Treasury inmates were less cutting in their overall verdicts. 'I thought you did a very good job,' said one of the more senior people. 'You caught something of the flavour, and the balance of interests and power and attitudes that are around, quite well. I wouldn't pretend to try and do the job myself and do it much differently.' Sir Douglas Wass expressed himself almost worryingly pleased. *But, Chancellor* coincided with his retirement. As his conscious gesture towards more open knowledge of how government works, it was, it appears, an acceptable swansong. According to one who knows him well, recently retired from the top of Whitehall, it also did him justice – although only, he surmised from his own long experience, thanks to some prudent forward-planning. 'I think you did get Douglas and Peter Middleton and Geoff Littler talking as they are. Douglas is, of course, a very cautious man, but all three of them are clever and in their own way cautious.

I did feel myself that they'd have sat around and said to themselves, "Look, we've got to be just a little bit careful about this. If we push our role too strongly, ministers are always very resentful of that. Besides, everybody thinks the Treasury are a lot of arrogant clever bastards pushing their weight around." So I think they were too self-deprecatory. They wanted that image to come over, and it did.'

They'd been helped in this, he thought, by our emphasis, which they echoed, on the uncertainties bedevilling economic management. 'That's true enough,' said this ex-mandarin, 'but at the same time they are actually compelled to say to ministers they should do so-and-so through the Bank or make this particular decision about interest rates. You could have followed up the contrast between the uncertain environment in which they're operating and the very certain, sure decisions they're compelled to take week in, week out.'

Perhaps the main criticism was that there were gaps in the series. Some of these we knowingly left, but others emerged only later. In different ways the selection of people to interview was questioned – both their rank and their field of work. In particular, one man said, we did not plunge low enough down the hierarchy. We had covered the key areas of work – the Budget, the international scene, and so forth – where the best people tended to work, but far more people were involved at less glamorous levels. 'Quite a lot of Executive Officers, Higher Executive Officers and Senior Executive Officers are doing an awful lot of work that never gets to ministers, and never is seen by an Under Secretary.' But their decisions could affect a lot of citizens. If one was talking about power, these were the people who had it. 'Take the Aid programme, or Health and Social Security, or almost any area of spending you care to name. There are all sorts of smallish problems which are the bread and butter of people in this place. There might be some difficult case where someone made a mistake in working out a pension or a redundancy payment, and it comes to the Treasury because it's slightly outside that person's delegated limits. It's a question of how well does the Treasury handle it? The programmes didn't catch that at all. It wouldn't have made particularly good radio, but that's a whole other side of the Treasury's work. When I was working on education spending as a twenty-five-year-old, I'd have cases like a tunnel collapsing under the University of Essex. How should the finance for that be handled? Should we pay the university money to compensate them for it? You'd never bother a minister with that, but it's quite important to the university concerned. And I'm not sure this sort of thing is all that small a part of the Treasury picture.'

There was another unbalancing omission, identified by one of the most senior men we talked to. We had underplayed the importance of Treasury economists. 'You gave almost no prominence at all to the very substantial amount of analytical work done by Terry Burns's staff. Rachel Lomax and others had their contribution, but they are, as it were, operational contributions to the actual business going forward. I don't think you picked up the fact that there are professional economic working papers published by the Treasury which are of interest to the academic world. They're analytical of the past in some degree, but of the future as well. There's quite a body of thinking and wisdom that comes up from that work, through Terry Burns himself. He's a very key figure in deciding which areas they're going to focus on. I don't think you reflected any of that.' Nor, added a more acerbic voice (from an academic econo-mist who's been in and out of government), did we report at all on how out of touch with the economics profession Treasury economists tend to be. They lived in a different intellectual realm, he thought, entirely dominated by pragmatism rather than the quest for truth. We hadn't explored that. On the other hand, we'd opened the eyes of at least some of his colleagues through the revelation (*see* pp. 71–2) that the Treasury model does receive a certain amount of political 'massage' before its results are published.

There weren't many out-and-out critics of the Treasury represented in the series. Naturally we had been anxious to find some. Radio journalism is not alone in being sharpened up by a few adversarial encounters. But there was a problem. Well-informed critics fell roughly into two classes: those who had attacked Treasury policies at different times over the past thirty years, and those whose professional formation and present interest were elsewhere inside Whitehall and who therefore might have institutional reasons for going into the attack. Neither group could be fully exploited within the confines of the programmes.

The first group could have been let loose if we had conceived a different series of programmes. But we were producing a snapshot not a movie. We were trying to show what the

Treasury was like at a particular moment in the early 1980s. To have opened up all recent economic policy to evaluation by the many first-hand participants doubtless willing to talk about it would have been a distraction from our scrutiny of the Treasury as an institution – besides requiring at least twenty-five episodes to tell. In a long article in *The Listener*[1] after the broadcasts, Sir Patrick Nairne homed in on this with telling effect. Welcoming Whitehall's willingness to open itself up again after *No, Minister*, he nonetheless regretted that the Treasury had managed 'to ward off the deeper value judgements about its powers and performance'. He could have done with more discussion of 'its successes and failures in recent years'.

What this comment perhaps reflects is the common feeling not only that the British economy has been a disaster area for a good many years but that the Treasury, as an ongoing institution, has been centrally responsible for this. But as we concluded in the series, the indictment against the Treasury must now be that it has too little, not too much, control over events. The failures may have been large (and sometimes the successes), but they have been attributable more to governments and political leaders, and above all to uncontrollable events, than to the Treasury as an institution.

The second class of critic – the insiders – was in baulk for more obvious reasons. Other Whitehall officials are unlikely to go on the record to offend their paymaster. We made some headway with Sir Frank Cooper, whom we interviewed just as he was retiring, and also, in more measured style, with Sir Kenneth Stowe. Politicians like Tony Benn also introduced a note of scepticism. But people with first-hand experience simply declined to unbelt. The foreign participants were almost as embarrassingly fulsome off the record as they were on the air. Most of the criticisms we heard depended on hearsay or rather distant judgement, and we were not prepared to use them, since we were trying to describe the place at first-hand. 'The criticisms that were made were weaker', a participant added, 'because they weren't from very penetrating people. You didn't seem to have got people who were close enough to be able to be more thorough.'

A flavour of what this criticism might have been came, tantalisingly, from a Permanent Secretary we went to see after the

---

1 12 May 1983.

broadcasts were over. He spoke now, as a listener, from behind an understandably dense cloak of anonymity. 'What I missed,' he said, 'was any examination of the scope for individual responsibility at the Treasury. I just have a feeling that they're sitting, as it were, in legal chambers, commenting on each other's comments, advising on each other's advice, and that all the big decisions, inevitably, are taken by ministers or by the Bank or by the real economy. I would make Kenneth Stowe's point (see p. 108) a little bit sharper by saying they're not in touch with the real world.'

This listener also felt we'd taken the Treasury too readily at its own estimation. 'Those comments of Michael Posner (see p. 24) and David Hancock (see p. 41) about the intellectual content of Treasury work and its exciting nature are a bit dangerous. I think everyone's arrogant, but what is the nature of the Treasury's arrogance? It's highly intellectual work, true. It's highly secret work, true. It's ostensibly concerned with big issues and big sums of money. But this inevitably produces a state of mind which has not been tempered by real individual responsibility. That would be my addition, my gloss, on what you said.' This was a point we could certainly have made more of. In private, senior officials made eloquent complaints about this very weakness in the typical Treasury career-structure – and at least one of our participants was actively seeking employment in the private sector not just because the financial rewards were greater but because it offered more personal responsibility. In the Treasury, ministers do take the most interesting decisions, and this eventually irks some of the ablest of their advisers.

There was something else we missed, which perhaps would only be seen in its full beauty by the custodian of a spending ministry, honed by years of battle with the controller of the purse strings. The Treasury's own method – its incessant quest for detached rationality – could, said this serving mandarin, in fact be turned against it. 'What the Treasury help me to do, because they insist on the right questions being asked and answered, is to ask and answer them ourselves. This is useful for our own purposes. Actually, the more you develop the case for doing something, the better the case is, and therefore the more likely you are to get the money from the Treasury. Rationality is a trap they fall into. It's not in the interest of the Treasury to be over-rational, because reason produces reasons for money. Their great new "financial management initiative" in fact has a

131

curious effect. It makes particular services define their objectives more clearly, and so it will lead psychologically, though maybe not rationally, to more pressure for more resources. If I were in the Treasury I would always want to feel I didn't understand the spending department's case completely, because that would in practice weaken its position. The Treasury score their greatest successes where it's not a matter of rational argument. Like at a bilateral meeting, when the Chief Secretary springs some sudden point you can't answer, and there's a million off your bid.'

The public spending programme was also, we suspect, the one where the Treasury itself had most reservations, feeling that we had not explored the full texture of this enormous preoccupation. 'I think it would have been interesting,' said one of them, 'if you'd done more to develop the argument on what we are really about. Are we just concerned with containing the totals, of all programmes or particular programmes? Or are we really concerned with output in cost-effectiveness, the yield on particular investments and so forth? There was a slight conflict of views between the Treasury participants on this. You'd put your finger on something there, with Anthony Rawlinson saying one thing (*see* p. 44) and Nick Sallnow-Smith saying something different (*see* p. 45), but you never took it up.'

And who was right?

'I think Sallnow-Smith was more right than Rawlinson, but not completely right. With our present administration, the Chief Secretary and the Chancellor are much more concerned with keeping the money down to tight levels and don't care very much on what it delivers. They say that's for the spending minister. I don't think that's quite the view of Treasury officials. They're brought up to take a longer view, and say it isn't only what goes in but what comes out. Tearing bank notes up in Parliament Square is not the same thing as building hospitals, but they may involve the same amount of money. We're concerned to get better value for money, we're concerned with cost-effectiveness. I think, if you like, the Rawlinson view reflects his proximity to our ministers.'

A similar kind of conflict of view arose close to home, in the critique of *But, Chancellor's* account of the Budget process. We had heard that the Chancellor himself, Sir Geoffrey Howe, was, in a good-humoured way, somewhat miffed at the impression the programme created (mainly by omission) that he, the Chancellor, was almost a stage extra, coming on at the last minute to deliver the Budget speech but otherwise unengaged in the Treasury's most fevered decision-making moment. This impression, if true, had been quite unintentional. One senior man later reminded us that it was also unhistorical. 'Increasingly Chancellors have got involved in Budget-making early on. I remember twenty-five years ago when the Chancellor would virtually sit in his room waiting for the great department to pronounce about the size and the shape of the Budget. This it would eventually do after the Permanent Secretary had chaired the Budget Committees, as they then were, and produced a set of recommendations. Modern Chancellors have wanted to get involved. They've been fretful as to what would finally emerge from the departmental process in the middle of February. Denis Healey was very much like that, and wanted to make a few speeches from the middle of January indicating what sort of Budget it would be. Geoffrey Howe has drawn it into himself even more than his predecessors.'

This point was endorsed by a less senior man who also thought we'd under-exposed the Chancellor. 'The shape of Howe's Budgets has been very much his,' he said. 'I mean, the emphasis on help for small businesses and the business expansion scheme and that kind of thing was his. That was where the impetus for them, and also for help for charities, came from. The impetus to drag those things out of the woodwork was his. He was very much the driving force. The work to put them in place and work out the details was officials'.'

But these two witnesses nonetheless slightly disagreed about whether or not the programmes gave a correct impression of how pervasively throughout the Treasury the Budget process impinged. 'There are hundreds of people around Whitehall beavering away on different bits of it,' the younger man said. The older hand thought the impression we gave was about right. 'I would say that if you actually went into a hundred rooms in the Treasury in the middle to end of February, you'd find that eighty-five of them were not dealing with the Budget at all. It's not all-consuming, if you're looking at the Treasury as a whole.'

Finally, there was the most elusive question of all – the really forbidden territory inhabited by civil servants and ministers in private conflict. There were flashes of this in the programmes for those who have been trained to crack the mandarins' code, but it wasn't something that those who'd been involved in were going to be very explicit about. Geoffrey Howe gave one version (*see* pp. 38–9). Another came later. How did the mandarins really cope with the ideologues? Weren't their habits of mind most disturbingly upset? Surely, we asked one Treasury man after the broadcasts, monetarist thinking became virtually *de rigueur* under Mrs Thatcher?

'Well, we've never actually had the thought police in,' he replied.

'You're not answering the question.'

'Well, Geoffrey has never asked me what I thought were the mechanisms by which the economy worked.'

'But is the Treasury really happier when government is quite certain what should be done?'

He paused reflectively, to formulate a proper mandarin's reply, asserting mandarin values without breaching the code which binds a civil servant not, in any circumstances, to criticise the government of the day. 'I think the Treasury generally, the civil service generally, would prefer quote undoctrinaire ministers unquote. I'm not making statements about this government, but I think civil servants tend to be people who want to look at the empirical evidence. They're pragmatists really. And to look at the success of policy in the light of its application. And to want to jettison it if it's wrong, intensify it if it needs to be intensified to secure the objections, without going back to some first principle.

'If you have a movement which says, you know, that the medium-term financial strategy is the only thing that matters, I don't think the Treasury is happy if it sees the medium-term financial strategy not working. And I don't say it isn't working. I mean I was just saying that that generally is the intellectual disposition of civil servants.'

And if the empirical evidence is at odds with the political objective? 'I'm not going to get on a soap box and say it in screeching tones. If you don't get the message, you don't get the message.'

Index